AR 8.
7pts. W9-DJQ-001

Coping with

MIGRAINES AND OTHER HEADACHES

Andrea Votava

THE ROSEN PUBLISHING GROUP, INC./NEW YORK

YA
616.8491
Vot
1997

Published in 1997 by The Rosen Publishing Group, Inc.
29 East 21st Street, New York, NY 10010

First Edition

Cover photo by Christine Innamorato.

Library of Congress Cataloging-in-Publication Data

Votava, Andrea.
    Coping with migraines and other headaches / by Andrea Votava.
        p.   cm.
    Includes bibliographical references and index.
    Summary: Discusses migraines and other kinds of headaches and what can be done to get rid of them.
    ISBN 0-8239-2566-8
    1. Headache—Juvenile literature. [1. Headache.] 1. Title.
RC392.V68   1997
616.8'491—dc21   97–31918
                                                                              CIP
                                                                              AC

Manufactured in the United States of America

About the Author:

Andrea Schregardus Votava is a freelance writer and editor currently living on the Mississippi Gulf Coast. Ms. Votava holds a bachelor's degree from Hope College and is a contributor to numerous books and periodicals.

Acknowledgments:

Many thanks to Carla Wilson for her help with researching this book. Thanks also to my family who supported me while writing this book and to my friends and colleagues who took time to share their stories with me. Special thanks to my husband, Brad, for his limitless patience, understanding, and encouragement in all my endeavors.

Contents

What Is a Headache?

Cheryl

Cheryl was really getting tired of having migraines. She had started to get them almost every weekend. The headaches felt like a jackhammer working overtime on the right side of her head. They were so painful that she had to cancel plans whenever they attacked. She hated missing time with her friends, but there was no way she could have any fun with a migraine. Plus, sometimes she threw up when she had a migraine and she didn't want anybody seeing that!

Cheryl's mom had taken her to see two different doctors for her headaches. The first doctor wouldn't give her any medication. He suggested that Cheryl was only saying she had a headache so she wouldn't have to go to school. That upset both Cheryl and her mother. Her mom also had periodic migraines and knew that Cheryl wasn't faking anything.

The second doctor thought that Cheryl most likely had migraines. This physician said that everything about her headaches fit the migraine pattern. He gave Cheryl some pills to stop a migraine when it hit, but so far the pills weren't working.

Her friends were asking questions about why she was always backing out of plans. Cheryl was scared

1

they wouldn't include her anymore, so she told them the truth. Now they all had suggestions for treating her migraines. At first Cheryl listened to their ideas. But some of them sounded pretty crazy. She doubted that changing her brand of lipstick would help, as her best friend had suggested. Other ideas actually frightened her, such as holding her head underwater during the migraine.

Her grandma thought that Cheryl had a brain tumor. She had been reading about pollution and said that Cheryl had probably been exposed to a toxic level of poison. Cheryl knew she hadn't been exposed to any more pollution than her brother, and he didn't have migraines. Sometimes, though, when she was lying in bed and her head was pounding, she thought about the possibility of a tumor. Or maybe cancer. It had to be something bad to make her feel like this.

Cheryl's mother was taking her to a different doctor tomorrow. Cheryl was pretty sick of all of it. She knew her family and friends meant well, but their advice was annoying. They all seemed to think they knew so much more about her pain than she did! She was tired of listening to them. She was tired of shuffling between doctors. She was tired of canceling plans. But most of all, she was tired of getting migraines.

More than 45 million Americans suffer from migraines or other headaches. These headaches can range from minor discomfort to crushing head pain. Most of these sufferers see their doctors each year about their head pain. Together, they spend more than 4 billion dollars on pain medication.

2

More than 157 million days of work and school are missed each year due to headaches. Countless additional days and plans with family and friends are cancelled.

Migraines and headaches are one of the most commonly reported ailments today. They are also one of the most frightening. Head pain can make even the most courageous person cower in a corner. There are no visible wounds to bandage—only invisible, crushing pain. Thousands of people are driven to their beds each day, wondering when the pain will end. Others try to get through a school or work day, often feeling sick and unable to concentrate because of the pain.

Trying to sort through advice from well-meaning family members and friends, different doctors, and advertisements for pain relief can be difficult. One of the best ways to try to cope with your head pain is to arm yourself with knowledge. Familiarizing yourself with your symptoms can help both you and your doctor treat your specific condition.

Understanding how scientists believe a headache works can also help significantly in trying to ease your suffering. It can help to know what a headache is a sign of—or what it is not. Understanding how a headache works can also aid in understanding different medication and treatment options.

A Headache

Pain is usually your body's way of warning you that something is wrong. But headache pain is different. Most headaches do not signal a brain tumor or other disease, even when the pain is severe. Often it is difficult to identify exactly what has caused the headache.

3

Many people, like Cheryl, receive a great deal of advice about how to treat their migraines or headaches. They also receive a lot of conflicting and confusing information about their headaches. Needless to say, coping with migraines and other headaches can be frustrating and upsetting. It's important to remember that you are not alone—there are others who are also suffering from head pain.

The most common types of headaches usually occur with no other symptoms. They develop gradually and have no distinct cause. These headaches generally disappear within a few hours, and have no lingering effects. Doctors call this type of headache a primary headache. Ninety percent of all headaches are primary headaches. The remaining 10 percent of headaches that are not primary headaches are symptoms of a larger problem or illness.

The National Headache Foundation has classified headaches into three distinct categories: vascular, tension, and organic. A vascular headache, of which migraines are the most common, are thought to be produced by the blood vessels in your head. Vascular headaches are discussed further in chapter 6.

Doctors are still learning about tension headaches. This type of headache produces a band-like pain around your head. It is the most common type of headache. Stress, fatigue, and depression may all contribute to a tension headache.

Organic headaches are headaches which *do* have an underlying cause. Organic headaches do not happen very often. Headaches produced by meningitis, a disease resulting in the swelling of membranes around the brain

4

and spinal cord, or an aneurysm, which is a weakness in a blood vessel wall, are examples of organic headaches.

Pain from a headache can be felt anywhere and everywhere in your head and can also affect your neck and shoulders. Headaches may occur sporadically and last only a short while, or they may occur frequently and be quite severe. Doctors label the short, infrequent headaches as acute, while the frequent headaches are called chronic.

What a Pain!

The symptoms and descriptions of migraines and other headaches can vary. One person's headache can be very different from another person's headache. Your head can ache in a variety of ways:

- ➯ Location: The pain can affect your entire head and neck, one side of your head, or just one spot.

- ➯ Severity: The pain may be mild and very manageable or so severe that you lose several days of work or school because of the headache.

- ➯ Frequency and duration: The pain can occur anytime. This pain can fluctuate from once in a great while to every day. The pain can also last anywhere from minutes to several hours or even days.

- ➯ Related symptoms: Nausea, vomiting, diarrhea, constipation, a tingling or feeling achy in different parts of the body, dizziness, and sensitivity to light and sound are some of the problems that may accompany the head pain.

5

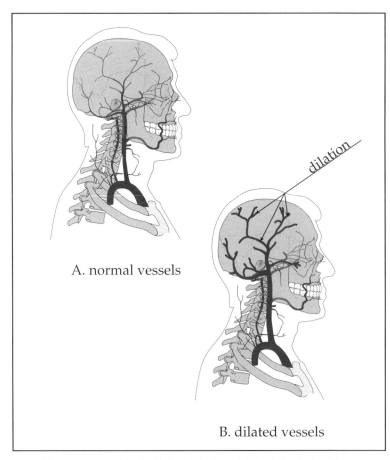

A. normal vessels

dilation

B. dilated vessels

Migraines are caused by the dilation of blood vessels in the brain, which can be seen in illustration B.

Migraines

Migraines are a special kind of headache and are in a class all by themselves. They are caused by the dilation, or enlargement, of blood vessels in the brain. Even though the pain of migraines is intense, they are considered primary headaches and do not indicate a brain tumor or other disorder.

6

Generally, migraine pain follows a pattern. A headache may be considered a migraine if at least two of the following statements describe it:

- The pain is worse on one side of your head than the other.

- The pain can be described as pounding or throbbing.

- You are unable to continue your daily routine.

- The pain gets worse with activity.

And one or both of the following statements describe it:

- You feel sick or feel like vomiting.

- Light or noises bother you more than usual.

It is possible to suffer from all of these symptoms, or even more. Only your doctor can give you an accurate diagnosis of migraines.

Migraines vary from person to person, but each sufferer usually has a warning period. The warning period may come the day before or just minutes before the head pain hits. You may just feel tired and out of sorts before the headache. You may also feel nauseous, have to vomit, and be very sensitive to light. Some people also experience trouble with their eyes, and see "misting" or zigzag lights in front of their eyes. All of these symptoms can last different amounts of time, from a couple of minutes to several hours.

When a migraine hits, the warning signs sometimes fade away. An intense, gripping pain may strike, which starts on one side of your forehead but then spreads to the center and back of the head. The migraine can leave you looking pale and sick, with bloodshot eyes and a runny nose.

Migraines are unpredictable. No one can accurately say how long the warning symptoms may last, how long the headache will stay, or when the next one will strike. But you can learn to predict when you are going to have a headache based on your previous experiences. This book will help you to understand when a migraine may occur, how to treat it, and how to prevent them in the future.

Who Gets Headaches?

If you experience headaches, you're in good, and crowded, company. Scientist Alexander Graham Bell, authors Edgar Allan Poe and Virginia Woolf, and past presidents Thomas Jefferson and Woodrow Wilson all are believed to have suffered from migraines. Other great figures from history who sought help for their head pain include composers Frédéric Chopin and Peter Tchaikovsky, Roman Emperor Julius Caesar, psychologist Sigmund Freud, and basketball star Kareem Abdul Jabar.

Anyone can get a headache, and most people do experience one at one time or another. Boys seem to get migraines as often as girls, but women get them much more often than men. Migraines most commonly begin during adolescence or during your twenties, and tend to disappear as you age. Experiencing migraines after age fifty is rare.

Migraines also tend to be genetic, which means you are more likely to have migraines if somebody else in your family also has them. About 60 percent of people who suffer from migraines have family members who also suffer from them.

When to See the Doctor

Many people are reluctant to see their doctor or ask for help when experiencing a headache. Since you can't see the cause of the pain, you may feel that your headache isn't serious enough for treatment.

Do your headaches interfere with everyday activities? Are you using more and more medications without feeling any real relief? Do you take medication even before a headache strikes out of fear that one will? Do your family and friends get upset when you miss more and more events with them? Your answers to these questions can help you decide if it is time for a doctor's help. Mild headaches at one time or another are quite common, and many do not require medical attention. If you have not eaten for several hours or did not sleep very well the night before, a meal or a nap may remedy your headache. Some over-the-counter medicine from the drug store may also help you.

If you keep getting headaches, however, and nothing you do seems to help, call your doctor. He or she can help you figure out whether your headaches are a temporary annoyance or a long-term condition that requires some form of treatment.

In the past, some doctors often didn't take their patients seriously and believed headache pain was "all in the patient's head." But not anymore. Specialized headache clinics now exist to help sufferers manage their pain and more doctors and clinicians are devoting their practices to the research and study of headaches.

It is important to take your headaches and migraines seriously. It is just as important to find a doctor who will also take them seriously. There are many medications and treatments available today that can provide relief. Some can even prevent future migraines and headaches from occurring. Although migraines cannot be cured, their pain can be greatly reduced. There is no need to suffer from head pain.

Migraines

Have you ever spent an afternoon playing ball or lying on the beach, squinting in the sun the whole time? The squinting might have given you a headache. But once you moved out of the sun, the headache probably went away. Some headaches don't disappear quite so easily.

It can be very hard to find relief from a migraine headache. A migraine headache is not a typical headache, and just as there is more than one type of headache, there is also more than one type of migraine.

The head pain from a migraine can be so intense that many people must stay in bed and are unable to tolerate any noise or light. Most people struck with a migraine are unable to concentrate or think very clearly during the attack. Migraine sufferers lose innumerable days from school or work, time spent with family, and other events important in their lives while trying to cope with the pain.

The most common symptom of any migraine is severe head pain. The pain is usually located on one side of the head, but it may spread to the other side. In fact, the word "migraine" means "half the head." The pain may be an intense pounding or throbbing in the forehead, temple, ear, jaw, or around the eye. Some people say it feels like a hammer banging inside your head. Most people are unable to stand any stimuli and must retreat to a dark, quiet room for relief.

Many migraine sufferers also have problems with motion sickness. They tend to have colder hands and feet than people who don't develop migraines. A person who is afflicted with migraines must endure an average of one to five attacks per month. Prescription medicine from a doctor is often required to stop the pain. A doctor may also prescribe other treatments for relief, such as relaxation therapy or biofeedback, a process by which the patient gains control over his or her body and the way it reacts to stress.

Lauren

Lauren could hardly wait. Her school symphony was performing that night. Lauren had worked hard, finally making it to first violin. As she put away her instrument after practice, she thought about what this performance meant to her. As a senior, this would be Lauren's last concert, and she had a solo. It wasn't a really big solo, but it was enough to warrant extra practices and time spent with her music teacher.

In addition to her music, Lauren had many other activities that demanded her attention. Graduation was coming up and there was a party almost every weekend. Plus, final exams were right around the corner. Lauren was trying to squeeze in as much studying as she could to raise her final grade point average. She hadn't slept much lately and had missed some meals.

"Hey, Lauren!" Lauren's best friend, Amy, called from across the room. "Do you need a ride home?"

"Yeah! I'm coming!" Lauren replied, as she walked

12

toward Amy. *"Do you want to grab a pizza? All of a sudden I'm dying for one of Papa V's pizzas."*

"You have a craving for pizza?" Amy asked. *"I thought you didn't really like pizza, especially Papa V's."*

"I don't like pizza that much. But all of a sudden I really want one. So let's go!" Lauren said, pulling Amy toward the parking lot.

Two hours later, Lauren sat on her bed, brushing her hair. Only an hour until showtime. She felt confident that tonight's performance was going to be wonderful. Then Lauren noticed a few flickers of light out of the corner of her right eye.

The light bulb must be going out in that lamp, Lauren thought. She continued to brush her hair and thought about which outfit she was going to wear.

Suddenly there appeared to be hundreds of pricks of light dancing in front of Lauren's eyes. Lauren began to panic. What was going on?

As the tiny lights disappeared, Lauren felt a small, piercing pain over her left ear. Then the pain got stronger. Lauren got really scared. What were those lights? Why did her head hurt? The pain quickly turned into a persistent throbbing that covered the left side of her head. She dropped her brush and grabbed her head with both hands. Lauren squeezed her eyes tightly shut and tried to swallow. Her head hurt so bad! What should she do?

Lauren's stomach began to clench. She suddenly felt nauseous and she knew she was going to be sick. She stumbled to the door and opened it. It was so hard to concentrate. She had lived in this house her whole life, and suddenly she couldn't remember where the bathroom was!

Lauren ran down the hall. She made it to the toilet just in time. She threw up several times and lay down on the bathroom floor. She was so scared. What was going on? Why was she in so much pain? Was she dying? Should she call 911?

The pain throbbed harder and harder, and it didn't seem to be letting up. Lauren was terrified. She started to cry. This pain was unlike anything she had ever experienced before. And then Lauren realized there was no way she could play in the concert that night.

Common Migraine/Migraine without Aura

A common migraine is the type of migraine that most people experience. It is characterized by an intense, stabbing pain on one side of the head and may spread to the other side of the head. The pain can be so severe that it causes nausea. You may also experience a tender scalp, dizziness, runny nose, diarrhea or constipation, "gut" pain, a dry mouth, and weakness or a "pins and needles" feeling in parts of your body. The pain can also cause shaking and an intolerance of any light and sound. Sufferers of the common migraine may also experience a prodrome. A prodrome is a warning that occurs several hours or even a day before an attack. These warnings may include a ringing in the ears, a sudden burst of energy, a craving for a specific food, excessive yawning, mood changes, or a cold feeling. The signals depend entirely on the person who gets the headache.

Often, a person in the middle of a full-blown migraine attack will feel totally out of control and panicked. The pain is overwhelming, and it is even difficult to think.

Common migraines can last from a few hours to several days and occur with a greater frequency than classic migraines.

Classic Migraine/Migraine with Aura

A classic migraine includes many of the same symptoms as a common migraine. A classic migraine is different, however, from a common migraine because there is a definite "signal" that the migraine is coming. This signal comes as an aura, which is a visual disturbance that begins about ten to thirty minutes before an attack, or the onset of a migraine. A person experiencing an aura may see flashing lights, spots, stars, wavy lines, color splashes, or waves in front of his or her eyes. The images may seem to shimmer, sparkle, or flicker.

Other people experiencing an aura may have blind spots, tunnel vision, or lose their sight for a short time. Usually the visual problems are worse in one eye. All classic migraine sufferers experience an aura. Lauren experienced an aura when she saw unexplainable points of light while she was in her bedroom.

Lauren also experienced a prodrome. Hours before the migraine hit Lauren, she wanted pizza, a food she didn't like very much. This craving was Lauren's prodrome.

During a classic migraine you may also experience weakness in an arm or leg, difficulty pronouncing words, confusion or dizziness, a tingling or "pins and needles" feeling in the face or hands, runny nose, sweating, and the need to urinate frequently. Some people also get a swelling in the ankles and wrists, a dry mouth, abdominal pain, and diarrhea.

A classic migraine may last from several minutes to one to two days. When the migraine is gone, most people feel very tired and drained.

Migraine Equivalent

A migraine equivalent has all the same symptoms as a classic migraine, including stomach pains, nausea, vomiting, confusion, mood changes, and auras or other sight problems, except there is no head pain. People experiencing a migraine equivalent do not get the intense head pain that is the standard for other migraines. Children and adolescents are struck more than adults with this condition. Headache specialists have theorized that patients with unexplained pain in the body, dizziness, and fever might be having a type of headache-free migraine or migraine equivalent. Young adults who have problems with migraine equivalents tend to experience classic or common migraines later in life.

Exertional Headache

This type of migraine occurs suddenly and is brought on by activities that increase the pressure inside your head. These activities include lifting weights, running, diving, sneezing, coughing, bending, and even sexual intercourse. The pain of an exertional headache starts at the beginning of the activity, and usually lasts a few minutes, although it can last up to a day. Some activities are more

16

likely than others to bring on exertional headaches. People who have recently begun a work-out routine also tend more than others to get exertional headaches.

There is a difference between benign exertional headaches and exertional headaches. If a doctor says you have a benign exertional headache, that means there is nothing life threatening about the headache. Other types of exertional headaches may indicate that there is something more to the pain. About 10 percent of exertional headaches indicate a problem. The remaining 90 percent of exertional headaches are benign and, even though they can be excruciating, are not a threat.

An exertional headache is not very common. Benign exertional headaches occur in a very small number of migraine sufferers. They are more prevalent in people who suffer from different kinds of migraines.

Familial Hemiplegic Migraine

In addition to the stabbing head pain of a migraine, familial hemiplegic migraine sufferers experience a condition known as hemiplegia, or paralysis on one side of the body. The paralysis is usually temporary, but it may take days or weeks to recover full control of your body. These people may also suffer from vision problems, a general feeling of dizziness, or a feeling that the room is spinning. A hemiplegic migraine is very rare, and evidence shows that it tends to be genetic.

Basilar Artery Migraine

Basilar artery migraine received its name because it involves a disorder of a major brain artery. This type of migraine is usually preceded by an aura. The piercing head pain associated with a basilar artery migraine is usually felt at the back of the head and on both sides.

People who are struck with a basilar artery migraine may also suffer before or during the headache from poor muscular coordination, double vision, a ringing in the ears, hearing loss, slurred speech, numbness in the arms or legs, and the feeling that the room is spinning. Basilar artery migraines may cause a brief (one to ten minutes) loss of consciousness.

Basilar artery migraine is more common in women than men and more common in teenagers than adults. This type of migraine is thought to be related to a woman's menstrual cycle. The sufferer feels an overwhelming desire to sleep and sleep does actually help. Basilar artery migraine is not a common type of migraine.

Ophthalmoplegic Migraine

Ophthalmoplegic migraine tends to attack people under thirty years of age. This rare type of migraine involves many sight problems. The pain from an ophthalmoplegic migraine is excruciating and severe, and normally occurs on one side of the head. There is often pain around one eye, a droopy eyelid, and double vision. When the head pain subsides, a sufferer may find that the muscles around the eye are paralyzed. The paralysis will usually correct itself after several days or weeks, but with repeated attacks it may take longer and longer to recover from the paralysis. An ophthalmoplegic migraine can be a very frightening type of migraine and is often mistaken for an aneurysm or a brain tumor.

Status Migrainous

Although a status migrainous headache does not signal an underlying disease, the pain and nausea are so severe that sufferers are most often hospitalized to bring the pain under control. A status migrainous begins much like other migraines, with powerful, throbbing pain on one side of the head. What sets this migraine apart from others is the length of the attack; a status migrainous can last more than seventy-two hours and even up to a week or more. Nausea and diarrhea may also be present during the entire headache and can cause severe dehydration. Status migrainous is a very rare and a very intense type of headache. People who get this type of headache often seem to be anxious and depressed before the headache strikes.

Dysphrenic Migraine

Many people who are prone to migraines are unable to concentrate or think very clearly during an attack, but people who suffer from a dysphrenic migraine are actually experiencing a severe mental disturbance. They may have amnesia, or a loss of memory, or be confused, agitated, and disoriented. These symptoms may occur with or without the pain of the headache. A dysphrenic migraine is not common.

Some of the migraine types discussed in this chapter are quite common, and some are a little more rare. Whatever kind of migraine or head pain it is that afflicts you, help is available. Keep reading to learn about other types of headaches and how to find relief.

Tension and Cluster Headaches

Marco

Marco glanced at the clock again. It was almost two in the morning. This was going to be his third night in a row that he got less than five hours of sleep. Marco could feel the stress level rising in his body. He was working on the final paper for his chemistry class and it was due in two days. It was assigned months ago, but Marco didn't think it would be so hard.

The words on the page of his book started to blur as Marco sat hunched over his desk. He decided to call it a night and go to bed. He wouldn't be able to accomplish anything when he was so tired.

The next day in class, the teacher announced that there would be an unscheduled exam the next day. Marco started to panic. There was no way he could study for the test tonight. He wouldn't finish his chemistry paper on time if he didn't work on it tonight. Marco started to feel guilty for letting his studies slide all semester.

As he walked down the hall toward his next class, Marco tried to stretch his neck from side to side. His best friend saw him.

"Marco, are you okay?" Tommy asked.

"Yeah. I'm just tired," Marco replied. "I haven't finished that chemistry paper yet and it's beginning *to catch up with me."*

"Well, don't forget that Friday is the dance. I told Samantha that we could count on you to get your father's car."

"Uh, sure, no problem," Marco faltered. "I've got to get to class. Catch you later."

Marco had forgotten about asking his father for the car. There was no way his dad was going to let him use it. Last time Marco had borrowed the car he had run into a mailbox.

By the time Marco got to his next class, he could feel a slow ache spreading around the top of his head. He was also having a hard time turning his head. Marco wondered how long this would last. It was five more hours until he could go home, but even at home he didn't have time to sleep or relax. The pressure was beginning to bury him.

Tension Headaches

"Tension" headache, like the one Macro had gotten in class, may not be the best name for this type of headache because it implies that only tension is the cause of the pain. Stress and tension can increase and intensify headaches, but they alone cannot cause a headache. Tension headaches are the most common type of headache. There are very few people who don't have tension headaches at least once in a while.

Tension headaches are much different than migraines. The pain in the majority of tension headaches is much less severe than that of migraines. Whereas a migraine can bring your world to a screeching halt, it is possible to function with a tension headache. The pain is still very real during a tension headache, but it is usually less debilitating. Sometimes tension headaches can actually trigger a migraine.

Tension headaches used to be called muscle-contraction headaches. They were so named because researchers once thought that the tensing and stretching of muscles in the neck, scalp, and face were the cause of these kinds of headaches. Scientists no longer think that is the case. They are now debating whether tension headaches are really a lesser form of migraines.

Episodic Tension Headaches

The most common kind of tension headache is an episodic tension headache. The pain from this headache is a dull, squeezing ache that usually begins gradually. It is often described as a tight band wrapping around your skull, or a cap pinching the top of your head. You may feel the pain around the forehead, scalp, or on the back of the neck. Most people who experience this type of headache feel as if their head is in a vise. They often find that they can't relax their neck or scalp muscles. An episodic tension headache is a tension headache that usually occurs no more than fifteen times per month.

The pain from an episodic tension headache is often felt on both sides of the head. This headache is usually mild, but can sometimes be severe. You may find yourself trying not to move your head or neck or holding your head in your hands to try to ease the pain. The pain may last only a few minutes or it may take several hours to disappear. Some people endure many episodic tension headaches in a row, and then the headaches go away for a long time.

The majority of people with episodic tension headaches do not experience such side effects as nausea and vomiting. In very severe cases, however, these side effects may appear. Many sufferers do have some ringing in the ears, slight dizziness, a sensitivity to light and noise, blurred vision, and a lack of alertness. An episodic tension headache can be aggravated by something as small as shivering from being cold.

The exact cause of an episodic tension headache is not known. Many things may contribute to it, including muscle tension, eyestrain, and poor posture from slouching over a desk. Contrary to popular belief, intense mental concentration cannot cause this tension headache.

Episodic tension headaches can usually be halted with over-the-counter pain medications, such as acetominophen (Tylenol), ibuprofen (Advil), or aspirin (Bayer).

Chronic Tension Headaches/Chronic Daily Headache

You may have chronic tension headaches if you begin to have a tension headache daily or almost daily for at least six months. These headaches are also known as chronic daily headaches. With this type of headache, there is a sensation of your head and neck being in a cast. The intense pain is felt on both sides of the head and can linger for weeks, months, and even years. The headache is there when you go to sleep at night and when you wake up in the morning. Chronic tension headaches are very different from other kinds of headaches, which are usually much shorter in duration. They can cause your scalp to become very sore—so sore that even combing your hair can hurt.

The daily pain of a chronic headache can wear you down.

As with episodic tension headaches, the cause of chronic tension headaches is not known. Muscle tension alone is probably not to blame. These headaches could be forms of migraines.

Chronic tension headaches often can be relieved with nonprescription drugs. However, it may take a great number of pills to stop headaches. And taking too much medication can actually cause another headache. Your doctor may prescribe medications to try to prevent these headaches. Preventing a chronic tension headache is often much easier than trying to relieve the pain after it starts.

Your doctor may try to help you figure out exactly what is causing your headaches. If you know what is causing them, you may be better able to manage the pain. Physical therapy, massage, and other relaxation exercises may also help the muscle strain that contributes to chronic tension headaches.

Combination Headaches

A combination headache occurs when the sufferer has both a migraine and a tension headache at the same time. A person who is experiencing tension headaches, with a dull, constant ache, may at the same time develop the severe, pounding pain of a migraine. Other symptoms of a migraine, including nausea and vomiting, may also occur.

On the other hand, a full-blown migraine, with its intense, jabbing pain in the head, may also bring about a

24

tension headache. A migraine will often aggravate the muscles of the neck and head to the point where a tension headache develops.

Cluster Headaches

A cluster headache is more intense and much more painful than even the most severe classic or common migraine. In fact, it has been called one of the most severe and excruciating pains known to humankind.

A cluster headache is a type of migraine and is named after its tendency to occur in groups, or clusters. People afflicted with cluster headaches usually have no aura or warning that an attack is about to begin. The cluster attack begins with mild pain around or through one eye or in the temple area. Within minutes, the pain becomes debilitating and spreads to that side of the face. The pain in the eye from a cluster headache is steady and piercing, and is much different from the pounding pain of other migraines. It is sometimes described as vicious, and can feel like an "eye is being pulled out." The eye during a cluster headache also becomes watery and red with a sagging eyelid. Sweating and a stuffed or runny nose usually accompanies the headache.

The pain from a cluster headache is so intense that most people cannot sit still during an attack and will often pace the floor or rock in a chair for hours. One cluster headache patient explains, "You can't lie down because you're so fidgety. The pain is unbearable." This is much different than experiencing a migraine, where the sufferer needs to lie still because of the pain.

25

The average cluster headache lasts approximately forty-five minutes, and can occur in clusters, or one right after the other, for a week or two. People are usually struck with cluster headaches between the ages of twenty and forty and men get them much more often than women. Roughly 1 million Americans suffer from cluster headaches.

Researchers have discovered that cluster sufferers have many similar physical appearances. The skin texture of most cluster sufferers tends to be coarse and can resemble an orange peel. Cluster headache sufferers are often heavy smokers and drinkers.

Cluster headaches may last from a few minutes to a few hours, and then they reappear. People with cluster headaches don't usually feel relief with the end of an attack because they know another one will be starting soon. Cluster headaches often start during sleep, usually beginning one to three hours after falling asleep, and the headache usually wakes the sufferer. Cluster headaches can happen several times a day or night for several weeks or months. Then they may mysteriously disappear for months or even years. People often suffer from cluster headaches in the spring and fall, leading researchers to believe they are linked to changes in the hours of daylight available in different seasons.

Although rare, chronic cluster headaches have been known to last for years. The pain may be very severe, but they do not cause permanent harm, such as brain damage. They also do not lead to other disorders. Cluster headaches are often misdiagnosed because they are so rare and because sufferers may only get them every few years. In fact, they are most often mistaken for sinus trouble. Some people suffering from cluster headaches have had teeth pulled, sinus surgery, or psychiatric treatment in an effort to cure the pain.

The sudden start and the short length of cluster headaches can make them hard to treat. Once the medicine has had a chance to start working, the headache has usually subsided on its own. There are several medications now available, most of which are in nose drop form, that have been relatively successful in treating cluster headaches.

Headaches as Symptoms

The number one reason that people seek medical attention for their head pain is because they fear a brain tumor. Most people believe that the worse the pain, the more serious the reason for the pain. A broken leg is more serious, and hurts worse, than a bruise on your shin.

Headaches are different. A migraine brings excruciating pain, but it is a fairly common complaint. Many people suffer from migraines, but headaches that are a symptom of a serious disorder are fairly rare. Some disorders that have headaches as a symptom include brain tumors, aneurysms, meningitis, and giant cell arteritis.

The few headaches that are symptoms of another problem should be taken very seriously. If you have any of the symptoms listed below, you should contact your physician immediately:

- Sudden, severe headache, often described as a "thunderclap"

- Headaches that increase in intensity, frequency, or duration

- Headache associated with convulsions or seizures

- Headache with a stiff neck, rash, numbness, weakness, or difficulty speaking

28

- Headache accompanied by confusion or loss of consciousness

- Headache, nausea, or drowsiness following a head injury, even just a "bump on the head"

- Headache associated with pain in the eye or ear

- Persistent headache in a person who was previously headache free

- Headache after a respiratory infection or sore throat

- Persistent headache that gets worse after sneezing, coughing, or straining

- Pain when bending your head forward

- Headache that interferes with normal life

Brain Tumor

The fear of a brain tumor drives more people to the doctor than the actual pain of the headache. In reality, brain tumors are relatively rare. Despite how bad your head hurts, most headaches are *not* brain tumors.

A headache that may indicate a brain tumor has pain that becomes worse and worse over time. This pain may come and go, or it may be continuous. The headache is generally nonspecific, meaning you may not be able to point to one spot on your head and say "It hurts *here.*" The pain can be all over your head. Most headaches caused by a brain tumor are made worse by things like coughing, straining, or sneezing. These headaches are also usually worse in the morning.

As a brain tumor grows, it can cause a headache by pressing on pain-sensitive blood vessel walls. The tumor might also press against the nerve tissue covering the brain, creating a headache. Contrary to what many people believe, a brain tumor can grow to be quite large without ever causing any problems.

Brain tumors often cause severe nausea and even projectile vomiting. Other symptoms of a possible brain tumor include seizures and problems with vision, speaking, and coordination. Someone with a brain tumor may also experience personality changes. Other people may notice a once easygoing person turning edgy and irritable. Treatment for a brain tumor usually includes surgery, radiation, or chemotherapy.

Aneurysm/Hemorrhage

An aneurysm is a weakness in a blood vessel wall. The aneurysm appears as a balloon-like bulge in the vessel. The blood vessel may slowly leak, or it may burst. If a blood vessel begins to have uncontrolled bleeding, it is called a hemorrhage. When an aneurysm in your brain ruptures, or begins to hemorrhage, it can lead to a stroke. A ruptured aneurysm can cause brain damage, paralysis, and death.

Aneurysms often feel like frequent migraines or cluster headaches. The weakness in the blood vessel wall is causing the pain. When an aneurysm bursts, it causes a sudden, unbearable, excruciating headache. A person with a ruptured aneurysm quickly loses consciousness.

If a doctor discovers an aneurysm early enough, he or she can operate before it becomes a problem. The weakness in the blood vessel wall can be corrected. Some aneurysms can be prevented by keeping your blood pressure under control. Your blood pressure indicates how hard your heart is having to work. If your heart is working too hard, it can put pressure on the blood vessels. Consult with a doctor about your blood pressure. Exercise, a healthy diet, and controlling stress levels can all help keep blood pressure down.

Sometimes head injuries can cause hemorrhages. A blow to the head can cause a blood vessel to bleed. Unlike a cut on the arm, bleeding in the head is hard to detect. If you have had a head injury recently and begin to feel abnormally drowsy or sick to your stomach, these could be signs of a hemorrhage. Other signs of a hemorrhage after a head injury include vomiting and pain when bending your head forward. Hemorrhages need medical treatment immediately.

Meningitis

A severe headache is one of the signs of meningitis. Meningitis is a disease caused by a bacteria which results in the swelling of the membranes, or meninges, that surround the brain and spinal cord. This inflammation is caused by an infection. Being exposed to meningitis or having a history of problems with middle ear infections can sometimes indicate meningitis. Often, however, it is contracted when someone is in direct contact with a person who has the disease.

There are two kinds of meningitis: viral and bacterial. Viral meningitis is caused by a virus and usually is not a life-threatening disease. It does need to be treated in a hospital and generally runs its course quite quickly. Bacterial meningitis, on the other hand, can be fatal. Bacterial meningitis is caused by bacteria and needs immediate medical attention.

One of the symptoms of meningitis is a severe and constant headache. Bending the head forward is often impossible because of the pain. Usually someone with meningitis runs a high fever and experiences nausea and vomiting. A very stiff neck is also a frequent complaint, and light usually hurts the eyes of someone suffering from the disease. Important clues in diagnosing meningitis are confusion, sleepiness, and difficulty in waking from sleep.

Meningitis is diagnosed through a lumbar puncture, or spinal tap. During a lumbar puncture, a long needle is inserted into the lower back. Fluid from the area surrounding the spinal cord is withdrawn. Testing this fluid can indicate the presence of an infection.

Meningitis is a serious disease that needs medical attention. As previously stated, some forms can be fatal. Most people usually make a full recovery from meningitis. If left untreated, meningitis can cause seizures, deafness, and mental disabilities.

Temporal Arteritis (Giant Cell Arteritis)

Temporal arteritis, also known as giant cell arteritis, is a serious, but treatable, condition. It is an inflammation of the arteries in your head that lead to the eyes, brain, and scalp.

A headache brought on by temporal arteritis is usually felt in the temporal region, or the area known as your temples. This kind of headache has been described as a burning, throbbing, and jabbing pain. There can also be pain when the person is chewing.

Symptoms of temporal arteritis include a lack of energy and feeling generally tired and ill. Someone with temporal arteritis may begin to lose weight for no reason. His or her temples may hurt when touched. Some people also lose vision in one eye. This blindness is often quite sudden, but usually temporary if treated immediately.

Doctors diagnose temporal arteritis by performing a test on your red blood cells. This test measures the rate at which red blood cells settle in a glass beaker over one hour. If temporal arteritis is present, the rate will be above normal.

Steroids are a usual course of treatment for temporal arteritis. Surgery is also often necessary to remove a part of an artery located near the temples. If the condition is left untreated, it could lead to permanent blindness and possibly a stroke.

Temporal arteritis is a rare condition, and young people do not need to be too concerned; the majority of people who contract temporal arteritis are over the age of fifty-five.

Is It a Migraine?

Headaches come in all shapes and sizes. All headaches differ in location, frequency, and intensity of pain. "I have a headache" is the number one complaint of most illnesses. This makes it very difficult for a doctor to establish exactly what kind of headache *you* have.

The pain from each kind of headache can be intense. Many people assume that if their heads hurt that bad, and they don't have brain tumors, then they must have migraines. Their headaches are very real, but they are seldom migraines. It is important that you allow a doctor to make the correct diagnosis about your particular headache. Then the right medication or treatment can be prescribed to treat your specific headache pain.

Allergies

The medical community has debated for years over whether allergies are a source of migraines. Many doctors say they are not. There is no doubt that allergies can make an existing headache worse, but it has not been proven that they can cause migraines. Even though doctors feel this way, many people with migraines believe they are wrong. Allergies can, however, cause a headache that is not a migraine.

34

First, it is important to understand exactly what an allergy is. Your immune system, the body's defense center, is responsible for fighting off infections. If the immune system detects an invader, like a bacteria or virus, it mobilizes its troops against the attacker. The immune system's biggest weapons are the proteins that it manufactures. These proteins are called antibodies. Antibodies are like self-guided destroyers. They travel through the bloodstream until they reach an invader. When the antibodies reach the invader, they attach themselves to it. This destroys the invader.

During an allergic reaction, the immune system begins producing antibodies. The allergic reaction happens when you are exposed to certain substances in the environment to which you are sensitive. These substances are called allergens. Allergens can be many different things, such as pollen from weeds, trees, grasses, and flowers. Allergens can also be household dust or molds. Allergies to foods are usually not a factor in causing allergy headaches.

If an antibody and an allergen come in contact with each other, a battle takes place inside your body. This clash results in the swelling of certain body tissues. The clash can also cause pain. For example, if an allergen and an antibody meet in your nose, you may wind up with a runny or stuffy nose and you may start sneezing.

An allergic reaction also sends a signal out to other parts of the body. The signal lets the body know that there is an invader. Other parts of the body may then start to react and defend against the invader. This is when you may develop a fever or feel achy all over. You may also get an allergy headache. An allergy headache may have the same intense pain as a migraine, but it is not a migraine. Usually allergy headaches are a nonspecific, dull ache over your entire head.

Often, people with headaches caused by seasonal allergies, such as hay fever, can find relief with allergy medications or nasal decongestants. These medications are available in prescription or over-the-counter forms. Someone suffering from a true migraine will probably not find comfort from these medicines. And, some people who are prone to migraines may actually get a migraine from certain chemicals found in allergy medications. If your allergies are very bad, your doctor may recommend a treatment that would include desensitization to the allergy.

Hangover Headache

After an evening of drinking too much alcohol, a person may wake up with a hangover headache. A hangover headache can feel the same as a migraine. Sufferers may feel a pounding on one side of the head. Nausea is also common.

A hangover headache is a direct result of the alcohol that was consumed. Alcohol dehydrates the body, which means that it sucks water from all body systems, including the brain. Blood vessels in your brain constrict, or tighten, as a result of this lack of water. These constricted blood vessels can cause pain.

Hangover headaches are often mixed headaches. In addition to the pain caused by constricted blood vessels, the pain may cause an involuntary tightening of the neck and shoulder muscles. This muscle contraction may contribute to a tension headache.

Despite what some believe, drinking more alcohol will not get rid of the headache. Caffeine may also worsen the pain.

The only way to prevent a hangover headache is to avoid alcohol. However, if a hangover does occur, drinking a lot of liquids (especially water) should help. This will rehydrate the body, or replace the fluids lost from alcohol. Over-the-counter pain medications, such as Tylenol or Advil, can also ease the pain.

Sinus Infection

True sinus headaches from a sinus infection are not common. Many people often think they are having a sinus headache because they have pain on one side of their head that often radiates to their face. Sinus problems do afflict about one in eight Americans, but most headaches are caused by other problems. Only your doctor can determine if you have a sinus infection.

To understand sinus infections and sinus headaches, it helps to be familiar with the sinus cavities. Your sinus cavities are hollow, air-filled spaces located in the bones surrounding the eyes and nose. There are four pairs of sinuses in the cavities. They are found behind your nose, underneath the cheeks, between the nose and the eyes, and over the eyes. The sinus cavities all connect to the nose through small pathways. These pathways can become blocked from allergies or infections. These infections can cause facial pain and sometimes headaches. A sinus infection is also known as acute sinusitis.

A true sinus headache has steady pain and soreness over the infected cavity. There is also an intense, dull ache that hurts worse when you move your head. Sinus infections may also result in a runny nose, fever, and some pain in one ear. Your face may swell around the infected area. It may even hurt to touch your face. Unfortunately, migraine headaches can also produce these same symptoms. This is why some people mistakenly think they have a sinus headache when they actually have a migraine. A doctor will need an X ray to show the blocked sinus and make the correct diagnosis.

Treatment for a sinus headache includes destroying the infection or treating the allergy causing the infection. Treatment is usually a pain medication, such as aspirin, as well as an allergy relief pill and a decongestant. Acute sinusitis will also need an antibiotic, such as penicillin, to treat the infection. People that are diagnosed with chronically congested sinuses often undergo surgery on their sinuses to relieve pain and headaches. There is no preventative treatment for sinus headaches.

Temporomandibular Joint (TMJ) Disease

Some people who have severe head and facial pain may think they have a migraine when they really have temporomandibular joint disease, or TMJ. TMJ is an abnormality of the temporomandibular joint, which is located between the temporal bone (found above your ear) and the mandible, or lower jaw bone. The temporomandibular joint is the only moveable joint in your head. TMJ disease is known to produce headaches in some people.

TMJ can cause severe pain on one side of the head. The pain may spread out to the jaw, neck, and behind the ear.

Sometimes there is a clicking noise when the jaw is opened. When the pain in the jaw becomes intense, a person with TMJ may not be able to chew with that side of the mouth, so he may use the other side. This aggravates the TMJ problem and the pain spreads. Because the pain is centralized on one side of the head, many people believe it is a migraine when it actually is not.

Your doctor can examine your temporomandibular joint. A physician who diagnoses you with TMJ disease may refer you to a dentist who is familiar with the condition. Studies are still being conducted to determine exactly what causes TMJ and how it can be treated. Your dentist may recommend you don't eat certain foods to ease the pain. Hot packs or heat applied to the jaw or massaging the affected areas may also help. Pain relievers, such as ibuprofen, can ease some of the pain. Your dentist may also want to use a dental splint or, in extreme cases, perform surgery to treat your TMJ.

Michael

The car was parked in the driveway. Michael had bought it with his hard-earned savings. The best part was that now that he had a car, he no longer needed to beg his parents to borrow their car. Life would definitely be easier, Michael thought.

Michael jumped into the car and headed down the road. He was going to pick up his girlfriend, Aimee. They were going to spend the day at the beach and then head to a party that promised to be great.

Driving down the road, Michael was startled when a dog darted from behind a bush and into the street.

He quickly slammed on his brakes to avoid hitting it. Michael missed the dog but wasn't so lucky himself. The driver behind him tried to stop, but wound up hitting Michael's rear bumper. The impact wasn't intense, but it gave Michael quite a jolt. He sat for a moment and tried to collect his thoughts. The driver of the other vehicle quickly ran over to Michael's car.

"Hey, are you all right?" the man asked.

"Yes, I'm fine," Michael answered. "Just a little shaken up."

Michael and the man surveyed the damage. Both cars had some scrapes and dents, but there wasn't any major damage. Michael and the other driver traded insurance information. Neither thought there would be any lasting problems and that their insurance should take care of everything.

Michael got back into his car. He felt bad that his new car was already banged up, but it could have been worse. The rest of the day would be better. Michael drove off toward Aimee's house.

The next morning, Michael woke up with a terrible headache and felt sore all over. I must have been jolted more than I realized, he thought to himself. But why would I have this headache? I didn't hit my head at all. Michael went to the medicine cabinet and took a couple of aspirin. That should take care of it, he thought.

Within an hour, most of Michael's body aches had vanished. The aspirin had worked well for that. But his headache persisted. His dad insisted on taking him to the doctor.

The doctor ordered a few tests to be done on Michael's head. She wanted to make sure there wasn't any serious damage, like a concussion or any bruising or swelling to Michael's brain. To Michael's relief, all of the tests came back normal. His headache, however, was still very painful. The doctor gave Michael a prescription for pain medication and asked him to come back in a week.

Michael took the prescription and headed home. He wasn't so sure the doctor knew what she was talking about. If he wasn't really injured, then why did his head hurt so much? Michael began to think that maybe he really was hurt. His dad told him that he was sure everything would be fine. But Michael was still scared.

Later at home, Michael took one of the pills. An hour later he realized that the headache was gone. He was still scared, however, that he might be more injured than the doctor realized. Michael felt another, smaller headache the next morning. He took a pill and again the headache disappeared.

By the time one week had passed, Michael hadn't experienced any more headaches. He also realized that with the disappearance of his pain, his fear had also subsided. He now believed the doctor when she told Michael that he would be fine.

Post-Traumatic Headache

A post-traumatic headache is a headache that is the result of trauma or injury to the head. You may get horrible headaches even if you've only had a slight bump on the head. An accident in which your head is not even struck or hit directly, as in Michael's minor car accident, can still cause painful headaches.

41

Post-traumatic headaches generally disappear within a few days to several weeks. In more severe injuries, the pain can bother you for months, years, or even the rest of your life. Sometimes people do not develop a post-traumatic headache for months following the incident. However, the majority of post-traumatic headaches usually begin within hours of the injury. If the headaches continue for more than eight weeks after the incident, it is then considered a chronic post-traumatic headache.

In addition to head pain, people suffering from post-traumatic headaches may become dizzy or lightheaded, have a ringing in the ears, or experience nervousness, fatigue, or sensitivity to noise and lights. There could be personality changes, such as becoming easily frustrated or angry, as well as depression, irritability, memory loss, a lack of motivation, and difficulty in concentration.

There also tends to be neck pain and muscle tenderness with a post-traumatic headache. Physical therapy may help with the neck and muscle pain. It may also help to relieve some of the head pain. Injury to the head is a frightening experience that can bring about anxiety, stress, and fear. This in turn may intensify, or worsen, existing headaches.

A post-traumatic headache can range from mild to severe. Because of the wide range of accompanying symptoms, sometimes friends, family, and coworkers think a person with a post-traumatic headache is making it all up. But he is not. The skepticism of others can lead to more stress and more intense headaches for the victim.

Often, post-traumatic headache sufferers will find relief through the use of simple pain medication, such as

42

aspirin, ibuprofen, and naproxen. Sometimes a doctor will also prescribe a muscle relaxant. For more severe, chronic headaches, a preventative drug may be prescribed. A preventative medication is a drug that can help to keep headaches from occurring. The most commonly prescribed preventative drugs for post-traumatic headaches are amitriptyline and beta blockers.

It may also help to talk to a therapist about any fears that may exist about the accident and subsequent head injury. Biofeedback and relaxation therapy may also help. The important thing to remember about a post-traumatic headache is that it usually does go away over time.

What Causes Headaches?

Many illnesses have an underlying cause. Pneumonia is caused by an infection. Severe stomach pains can be caused by a ruptured appendix. But headaches themselves are not a sickness. They are common in a majority of illnesses, but they are only a small part of these conditions and occur with other symptoms.

For many years, doctors thought they knew the cause of headache pain. They believed that tightening or tensing of the facial, neck, and scalp muscles were the cause of headaches. Some believed that intense mental concentration could cause head pain. Doctors also blamed an inability to deal with stress as a cause. Stress and muscle tension can certainly aggravate a headache, but they alone cannot cause one.

Doctors today believe that some blame may lie in chemical imbalances in the brain. They also believe that there may be a disorder in the way some people's brains and blood vessels work. This might make them more susceptible to headaches.

Unfortunately, all of the information that doctors and scientists have about headaches and migraines are theories. There is no definite answer about what a headache really is. More and more researchers are beginning to explore the science of headaches and what to do about

44

them. New theories are being presented and studied. The progress that is being made in determining how a headache works is leading to new and improved treatments.

Control Central

The human brain is an amazing system that relies on both nerve impulses and naturally occurring chemicals that control the body. Nerves are pain-sensitive fibers found within your body. Nerve fibers connect your nervous system and your brain and spinal cord with other organs in your body. Nerves allow you to feel different sensations both within and outside of your body. If you slam your finger in a door, for example, nerves in your finger sense the injury. These nerves are activated and quickly relay a message, or impulse, to your brain, where the sensation of pain is recognized. The signal that your brain receives is decided by where the activated nerve is located in the body. When you hurt your finger, the brain will recognize that the nerves in the finger are the ones being activated.

Many of the nerves in your body are located in your head. There is a network of nerves that cover the scalp. Some nerve fibers are found in the head muscles. Other nerve fibers are found in blood vessels located along the surface and base of your brain. There are also many nerves in the mouth, throat, and face. All of these nerves may contribute to the pain felt during a headache or migraine.

Nerve impulses travel from all over your body to your brain, much like a message relayed over a telephone wire. Nerve cells do not form a direct, connected line, and gaps

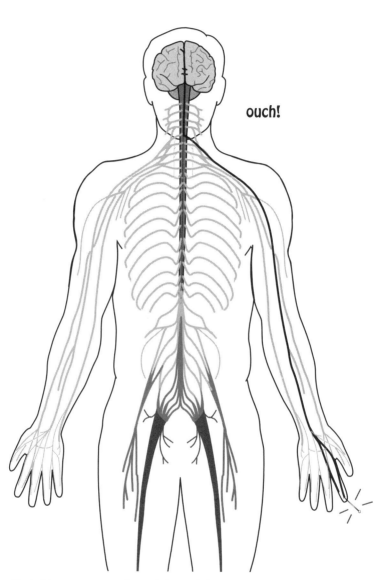

ouch!

The body's nervous system relies on the brain, which acts as its "control center." When pain is inflicted on any part of the body, millions of nerves react to send the pain message through the body to the brain.

exist in the network. Chemicals in the nerve network bridge these gaps and help to carry the message. These chemicals are called neurotransmitters.

Neurotransmitters are a vital link within your brain. They are used over and over again to help keep your nervous system working. Once neurotransmitters are released to relay the message they have been given, they are quickly pulled back and returned to the interior of the nerve cell. There the neurotransmitters are "wiped clean" to prepare for the next message.

Many scientists now believe that neurotransmitters are much more than simple messengers. These chemicals may actually affect many different systems in your body and an imbalance of these chemicals could cause problems. Some medications for migraines and other headaches are able to interfere with the recycling of some neurotransmitters. Doctors believe that this interference can balance the chemicals and stop head pain.

The Role of Serotonin

One of the neurotransmitter chemicals found in the brain is called serotonin. Serotonin aids in the communication between brain cells. It is also known as a vasoconstrictor, which means that it is able to constrict blood vessels. In addition, serotonin has been implicated in migraines and other headaches.

Serotonin works along the trigeminal nerve system, which is the major pain pathway within your body. It originates in the brain stem and moves along blood vessels as it spreads into your head and face. The trigeminal nerve

47

system's job is to convey nerve impulses from your face and head back to your brain.

Scientists are studying one theory that the nerve impulses in some people may become jumbled along the trigeminal nerve. The impulses may end up at blood vessels in the brain's protective covering and in the scalp. These blood vessels relax, fill with blood and become inflamed, or swollen. Nerve endings found in the brain covering and in the scalp are then activated and send a message of pain to the brain. A headache results.

The swelling of the blood vessels and the pain that results may be caused by changes in the brain's levels of serotonin. Research has shown that during a headache or migraine, serotonin levels drop. The drop in serotonin would make it possible for blood vessels to swell because serotonin helps to keep them constricted. Some researchers also believe that there are serotonin receptors in the lining of the stomach. The changes in serotonin levels during a migraine may also affect these receptors in the stomach. The result may be the nausea that so many people experience with their migraines.

There is much support for the serotonin theory. The best research lies in the people who experience migraines, and many of them find relief with medications that affect serotonin levels.

The female hormone estrogen has also been shown to influence serotonin levels. This may be one reason that so many more women than men have migraines. It may also be a reason why so many women have migraines around the time of menstruation, a period in which estrogen levels change.

48

Natural Painkillers

Endorphins are naturally occurring chemicals found in your brain. They play a major role in how we feel pain. Endorphins are our natural painkillers.

Your brain has an automatic pain control system. Researchers believe that this pain control system affects how much pain we feel. Endorphins are the chemicals that allow the pain control system to work.

Endorphins are thought to work by changing the relay of nerve impulses from one nerve cell to the next. How little or intense the pain is depends on the change that endorphins make between nerve cells. Your endorphins can stop a simple stub of your toe from feeling like a brick was dropped on your foot. One theory suggests that people who get bad headaches may have lower levels of endorphins in their bodies than other people.

Scientists are learning that endorphins cannot perform properly unless neurotransmitters are at their correct levels. They believe that during a migraine attack, the brain is busy using all available serotonin and other neurotransmitters to convey messages of pain. As the levels of serotonin drop, the endorphins are not able to function, and endorphin levels drop. When the levels of endorphins drop, there is nothing in the body to stop the pain.

There are ways of stimulating your body to produce more endorphins. Aerobic exercise, such as bike riding or jogging, is one way to increase your body's endorphin levels. What many people think of as a "runner's high" is actually endorphins flooding your body. The release of so many endorphins gives many people a sense of elation, or of being "high." Laughing, falling in love, and pregnancy are all believed to produce more endorphins. Stimulating production of endorphins at the beginning of a mild migraine or other headache may help to relieve much of the pain.

The Vascular Theory

The term "vascular" refers to the system of blood vessels within the body. The vascular theory of headaches, developed in the 1940s and 1950s, states that blood vessels inside and surrounding the brain are the cause of headaches. Doctors and researchers who believe in the vascular theory assert that when blood vessels outside of the brain dilate, or swell, they cause blood vessels inside the brain to constrict, or tighten, which can cause a headache.

Vasoconstriction is a term referring to the constriction of the blood vessels inside the brain. Vasoconstriction temporarily reduces the blood supply to parts of the brain. This constriction also results in a reduced supply of oxygen to the brain. Because of the lack of blood and oxygen to certain parts of the brain, a headache or migraine may result.

When the constricted blood vessels begin to relax, they fill with blood and may press into the brain and the underside of the skull. The vascular theory states that when the blood vessels begin to swell, they compress nerves. The nerve endings are continually activated and send messages of pain to your brain. This may account for the throbbing feeling of pain.

When activated, nerves within your head may also release chemical compounds that intensify pain. It is believed that some of these compounds may actually

50

lower your tolerance for pain. This would make your head hurt even more.

Many researchers who believe in the vascular theory think that the aura and prodromes associated with a migraine appear during vasoconstriction. They believe that headache pain actually begins with the refilling of blood vessels. This opposes the serotonin theory, which concludes that the swelling of blood vessels causes an aura and the constriction of the same vessels causes pain.

The vascular theory is supported by research. There are documented changes in the blood flow of people who are having a migraine or other type of headache. The theory is also supported by the fact that many of the medications that act so well in stopping migraines and other headaches work directly on blood vessels to stop their constriction and dilation.

There are, however, some problems with the vascular theory. For example, it does not explain the nausea that often occurs with migraines. It also does not explain the sensitivity to light and sound. Some researchers are quick to point out that everybody's blood vessels dilate in hot weather to prevent dehydration, but not everybody gets a headache.

It's in the Genes

Many doctors and researchers have long accepted that migraines seem to be genetic. More than 60 percent of people suffering from migraines have said that a close relative also suffers from them. In addition, certain people do seem to be more genetically disposed to having migraines than other people. Scientists are presently conducting research on certain types of migraines to find a way to pinpoint the exact chromosome that may be responsible.

Some doctors and scientists believe that everyone has a certain tolerance level within the brain for stressors, or things that cause stress. Stressors can be internal or external. You may or may not be able to control the stressors in your life.

One theory asserts that while migraines are a genetic condition, people who experience migraines also may have a disorder within their nervous systems. Researchers who support this theory believe that there are many more symptoms of a migraine, in addition to the head pain and nausea, that go unnoticed. One of these symptoms may be related to the electrical activity in your brain.

There is a great deal of electrical activity happening in your brain at any given time. Different parts, or regions, of your brain are responsible for all of your senses and functions. One part of your brain is in charge of whether you can carry a tune. Another part of your brain controls your jump shot. Electrical charges in your brain allow the different regions to function. Electrical charges contribute to all parts of your body, including walking, talking, chewing, and thinking.

Part of this theory alleges that there may be an abnormal burst of electrical activity in the brain that stimulates many different areas of the brain at one time. These areas would not normally be stimulated at one time. The eruption of electrical activity may also disturb the nervous system.

The abnormal electrical stimulation may be responsible for triggering the nausea and vomiting that may occur during a migraine. The nervous system disturbance may also lead to the weakness, lack of coordination, and numbness experienced during a migraine. The electrical burst may also be responsible for the aura experienced during a classic migraine. The electrical activity may stimulate certain areas of the brain to make you believe you are seeing shapes and lights that aren't really there.

Stimulation of a variety of areas in the brain may also account for other odd changes that may occur with a migraine. Some people may feel very happy or angry for no apparent reason right before a migraine strikes. Other people get very hungry. The dysfunction of the electrical system of the brain may be at fault.

This theory also states that the burst of electrical activity may set off a chain reaction. A spark in one area of the brain may set off a spark in another area. More and more areas of the brain are stimulated to respond. Some of the electrical activity may release certain chemicals which can compound the sensation of pain. The release of these chemicals may also prolong the pain.

Spreading Depression

The spreading depression theory of migraines is a combination of ideas. It states that irregularities may exist in certain people's blood vessels and nervous systems, and that these irregularities cause them to experience migraines. Researchers who support this theory think that a migraine is the result of a wave of decreased electrical activity in the brain.

There is constant electrical activity occurring in the brain. Electrical impulses firing in the brain allow us to do things such as type on a keyboard, solve math problems, or paint pictures. The spreading depression theory of migraines suggests that there is a gradual wave of decreased electrical activity that starts at the back of the brain and moves toward the front. This wave of decreased activity is known as the spreading depression.

Supporters of the spreading depression theory also believe that there is an instability in the blood vessels in some people. This instability would allow the walls of the blood vessels to expand and contract quite easily. If the blood vessels contract, there is a drop in blood flow through the vessels.

Research has also found that following the spreading depression, there is also a drop in blood flow in the brain. (Whether this drop is a direct result of the spreading depression is still a mystery.) The brain does strange things when it is deprived of blood and the oxygen found in the blood. The aura phase of a classic migraine may happen during this time of decreased blood flow.

There have been recorded increases in blood flow to the brain during the pain phase of a migraine. Although only sufferers of a classic migraine may experience a drop in blood flow before a migraine, sufferers of both classic and common migraines experience the increase of blood flow during the actual headache.

The spreading depression may be responsible for some of the other symptoms that occur before and during a migraine. Symptoms are affected by which part of the brain experiences the decreased electrical activity. For example, if the frontal lobes of your brain, which control thinking and concentration, experience the spreading depression, you may have a hard time concentrating or complain that you feel "out of it."

As mentioned earlier, the trigeminal nerve system is the major pain pathway within the body. The trigeminal nerve sends messages of pain through the brain stem and into the brain. Once in the brain, the messages are decoded and translated into "Ouch!" Part of the spreading depression theory says that there may be abnormalities along the trigeminal pathway that contribute to a migraine.

Both the changes in blood flow and the decreased electrical activity may also stimulate a host of other problems. Chemicals that are associated with pain in the body may be unleashed into the trigeminal pathway. This constant dumping of chemicals activates even more pain receptors in the brain. The result can be a constant, pounding pain. The chemicals also continue the cycle of constricting and dilating blood vessels. The pain response in the brain may be activated long after any stimulants are removed.

The spreading depression theory supports the belief that headaches may initially be stimulated by certain triggers. These triggers are substances to which certain people may be sensitive. Some common triggers include changes in the weather, alcohol, food additives, and stress. Triggers are discussed in detail in the next chapter.

Triggers

One of the first and most important steps in managing migraines and other headaches is to determine if there is a specific substance or activity that is causing your pain. Determining what sets off a migraine or other headache can be a very sensitive subject. Chances are, if you suffer from head pain, you've heard "Don't worry so much," or "You should learn how to relax." These are common phrases from people who just don't understand the frustration and pain of a headache.

Just as doctors are unable to explain fully what happens during a headache or migraine, they are also unable to explain exactly what starts a headache. They do know that in some people certain factors, or triggers, can start a headache. A trigger is something to which you are sensitive and provokes a headache attack. Triggers are very different from person to person, and they don't actually cause the pain. They stimulate different chemicals and mechanisms in your body that in turn cause head pain.

Triggers can be a wide range of things, including foods, odors, emotions, and things heard or seen. Different people have different triggers; peanut butter may trigger a headache in you, but not in anyone else you know. When a trigger is a food or smell or something else in your surroundings, it can be easy to avoid. There are some triggers that can't be avoided, such as a woman's menstruation.

A headache diary is one of the best ways to figure out what your triggers are. This will help you to avoid foods and situations that bring about your headaches. Chapter 8 explains how to keep a headache diary.

Food

Food-provoked headaches are probably not the result of an allergy to the food, but rather a sensitivity to chemicals found in the food. This means that you may not be allergic to a hot dog, but rather are sensitive to a particular chemical found in it. For many people, a certain food is a very powerful headache trigger. It is important, however, to not become overly concerned about your diet. It may be impossible to find out exactly what is causing your headaches and migraines. A sensitivity to a food may be only one of several things that triggered the attack. And you might have a reaction to a certain food one month and not the next. The headache or migraine may begin right after eating a particular food, or it can take hours for the reaction to occur.

Missing a meal is a very common trigger for people who suffer from migraines and other headaches. For this reason, it is very important for people who are headache prone to make sure they eat at least three times a day. Breaking your food intake into five small meals a day has been proven to be very effective.

The following list contains some foods and beverages that have been shown to trigger migraines:

Common Triggers	Less Common Triggers
Beans (broad, garbanzo, lentil, navy, pinto, pole)	Bananas
Beer	Bread (sourdough)
Bread, white	Buttermilk
Caffeine	Cheese (processed;
Champagne	American, cheese,
Cheese (aged; bleu,	cottage cheese,
brie, cheddar, colby,	cream cheese)
mozzarella, parmesan, romano)	Cocoa
	Eggs
	Figs
Chocolate	Fruit (citrus)
Milk (whole)	Juices (fruit)
Nuts (dry-roasted)	Liquor
Olives	Nuts
Peanut butter	Pickles
Peas	Sauerkraut
Processed meats	Seeds
(bacon, bologna,	Sour cream
ham, hot dogs, luncheon meats, marinated meats, pepperoni, salami, sausage)	Soy sauce
	Wine (white)
	Yogurt
Soft drinks (cola)	
Tea	
TV dinners	
Wine (red)	

Chocolate

Chocolate is an unusual trigger, because doctors and researchers are not sure whether chocolate causes an attack or can help to relieve one. In some people, chocolate is a trigger. In others, a sudden craving for chocolate may indicate that a migraine is about to strike. And yet in other people, chocolate may actually help to get rid of a mild headache. A food record can help to determine how chocolate tends to affect you.

Caffeine

Caffeine is another unusual trigger. Small amounts of caffeine, whether alone or combined with some medications, have been known to get rid of headaches. For other people, caffeine is a powerful trigger of headaches and migraines.

Some people who consume a great deal of caffeine may become dependent on it. By ingesting so much caffeine, your body continually wants more. If it doesn't get enough, withdrawal symptoms start. These symptoms include severe headaches. This is why people who are heavy coffee drinkers have a "caffeine headache" until they drink their first cup. In addition to soft drinks and coffee, caffeine is also found in chocolate and tea.

Additives

Many processed foods contain chemicals that enhance the flavor or keep the food fresh. Nitrites are a common chemical additive found in many packaged meats, including hot dogs and prepackaged lunch meats. The chemical phenylethylamine, found in chocolate, is often the culprit of headaches in people who have chocolate as a trigger.

Many people are also very sensitive to the naturally produced chemical tyramine. Tyramine is found in aged cheeses, red wine, pickled herring, bananas, and avocados. Tyramine has been found to affect several chemical processes in the body that are involved in migraines.

Monosodium glutamate (MSG) is an additive that is well known for causing many headaches. An MSG-induced headache has also been called the Chinese headache as it is a common additive in Chinese food. MSG can also be found on various food labels masked as autolyzed yeast extract, hydrolyzed vegetable protein, or natural flavorings. MSG can be found in broths, seasonings, whey protein, soy extract, malt extract, chicken, pork, or beef flavoring, smoke flavor, spices, meat tenderizer, seasoned salt, TV dinners, instant gravies, and in some potato chips and dry-roasted nuts.

Keeping a Food Record

The best way to find out if you have a food sensitivity that may be triggering your headaches is to keep a record. Write down each thing you eat or drink and write down the time it was consumed. Make sure to include any vitamins or medications that you are taking. Record all instances of headaches, including the time that they start. This may help to pinpoint a particular food that is inducing your headaches. For instance, you may have eaten a chocolate bar at 3PM on Monday, Wednesday, and Thursday. You may have noticed that you had a headache by 4PM on those days. On Tuesday and Friday, when you

60

didn't eat any chocolate, you didn't have a headache. You may stop eating chocolate and notice that now you rarely get headaches! Chances are, finding your triggers won't be that easy. But knowing them may well be worth it.

Hypoglycemia/Irregular Blood Sugar

Hypoglycemia is a common condition that can trigger a headache. If you are diagnosed with hypoglycemia, it means that you have chronic low blood sugar levels. Hypoglycemia often develops in people who have diabetes, but a person's blood sugar levels can also become irregular by fasting or missing meals. Irregularity can also occur by eating too many carbohydrates at once, such as breads, pastas, and anything with a lot of sugar, such as candy. Excessive sleep can also cause your blood sugar level to drop and bring about a headache. The key to avoiding low blood sugar levels or hypoglycemia is to maintain a constant regular blood sugar level in the body. One way to do this is by dividing your food intake into five small meals a day rather than three large ones. In this way, you can better regulate the amount of sugars that you eat. You will also avoid going too long without food.

Hormones/Menstruation

Women tend to suffer from migraines much more often than men, and attacks can take place before, during, or following a woman's period. The reason may be in their hormones. The female sex hormones, called progestin and estrogen, have been found to definitely play a role in triggering a migraine. Scientists and doctors are unsure what this role may be, but they do know that a migraine brought on by the menstrual cycle can be very intense and uncomfortable. Many women report that their "period migraines" tend to be much worse than others.

However, the number of young women that get migraines dramatically increases after menstruation. One theory of why menstruation triggers migraines has to do with the levels of estrogen in a woman's body. Estrogen levels tend to drop near the end of a woman's menstrual cycle. Estrogen may decrease the activity of certain nerve cells in the brain stem which use the chemical serotonin as a messenger. A decrease in the activity of these nerve cells means a drop in serotonin. Some researchers believe that an imbalance in the serotonin system of some people may cause a headache. Therefore, the change in estrogen levels during menstruation, by disturbing the serotonin system, may trigger a migraine.

Migraines triggered by menstruation can also be difficult to treat. Standard migraine medication may have little effect against a menstrual migraine. Starting a nonsteroidal anti-inflammatory drug (NSAID) three days before the headache is expected and continuing for the first few days of menstruation may help to prevent it. The anti-inflammatory drugs include ibuprofen (Motrin) and naproxen (Anaprox). Chemicals found naturally in the body, called prostaglandins, are partly responsible for inflammation that occurs in the body. The NSAIDs make it hard for the body to produce any prostaglandins. This may explain why NSAIDs may help stop menstrual migraines. Talk to your doctor about the best treatment for you before taking any medications.

Birth Control Pills
About half the women taking birth control pills today find that their headaches worsen after they start taking them. Other women find that their frequency of migraine attacks remains unchanged or even decreases while taking the Pill. Everyone's response is different, so it is recommended that women who have migraines should have a thorough discussion with their doctors about taking birth control pills or hormone supplements.

Pregnancy
Pregnancy also plays a role in the frequency of migraines. With most pregnant women, migraine attacks occur less frequently or disappear altogether when they are pregnant. This is true even in the last half of pregnancy, when estrogen levels are the highest. Unfortunately, most women find that their migraines return after giving birth.

Odors/Smells

For some people, certain smells are triggers, and these odors can be either pleasant or unpleasant. Many people are sensitive to the smell of cigarette smoke, for example, and it can often trigger a headache. The sensitivity can occur at any point, even in people who used to smoke. Gasoline, car exhaust, flowers, paint, certain foods, and aftershave are all common triggers. Some people cannot handle even a small whiff of perfume without getting a headache. Contrary to popular belief, it's usually the intensity of the odor, and not the smell itself, that is responsible for bringing about the headache.

Light

Bright light, such as sunlight or fluorescent light, is another common trigger. People who are prone to headaches often wear sunglasses to shield their eyes. The blinding light of the sun off a car windshield, snow, sand, or water can cause head pain. Any flickering light, as in the light in a room, strobe lights, a camera flash, laser shows, and computer monitors can also be triggers.

Loud Noises/Sounds

Loud noises can trigger migraines. These can be short, sudden noises, such as a firecracker or a car backfiring. Or they can be loud and constant noises. This could include a baby crying or the sounds of construction work.

Travel/Motion

Traveling can also act as a trigger. Most people are familiar with motion sickness, but don't realize that motion can also produce a headache or migraine. This could be from traveling in a car or on a plane, boat, train, or even on an amusement ride. Many people who are prone to migraines often suffer from motion sickness in their youth.

Generally, traveling takes you out of your everyday surroundings. Being taken out of what is familiar can disrupt your body. You may not receive as much sleep or get enough to eat. You may also experience a higher level of stress. All of these factors can contribute to a headache.

Weather Changes

Weather changes can bring about migraines or headaches in some people. Doctors' offices are often flooded with people complaining about head pain when there are drastic shifts in weather. Spring tends to trigger the most headaches, followed by fall. Other people are susceptible to the hot, humid days of summer. A migraine or other headache may be worse during these times, rather than more frequent. Thunderstorms, high winds, barometric pressure changes, sudden temperature changes, and exposure to extreme heat or cold can all trigger headaches.

Dressing for the weather can help you avoid some headaches triggered by weather. If it's very cold, dress in layers to stay warm. In summer, drink plenty of water to avoid dehydration. Stay inside when the temperature outside becomes extreme.

Stress

Stress is one of the best-known triggers of headaches. Any event that produces anxiety, such as a new job or an upcoming test, can bring on head pain. Big events, such as a family experiencing divorce or moving to a new city are easy stress triggers to spot. Everyday hassles and stressors are less easy to define. Yet constant pressures from school, the workplace, and home are the biggest headache triggers.

Long hours of studying or mental concentration can help to trigger headaches. Poor posture from slouching over a desk can bring about neck pain which can bring on a headache. Eyestrain from staring at a computer may also be a factor in triggering a tension headache. Tight muscles can trigger a combination of migraine/tension headaches.

Repressed or unexpressed emotions can also trigger headaches. If you are very angry or very sad and never "let it out," you can induce a headache.

During a stressful situation, certain chemicals, such as adrenaline, are released in the body. Adrenaline is a chemical found in your body that is responsible for raising your blood pressure. It also constricts blood vessels. Stress may bring about an imbalance of chemicals in your brain by raising the levels of adrenaline in your blood. The balance of these chemicals can provoke reactions in the brain that can cause a migraine. When there is prolonged or increased stress, adrenaline may be contributing to the frequency and severity of your migraine attacks.

Many people for whom stress is a trigger suffer from a migraine or headache after the stressful period is over. This is known as a "let-down" headache. Students and other people who are busy Monday through Friday, and are prone to migraines, often get hit with head pain on Friday night or Saturday morning. These headaches occur because once the stress level is reduced, blood vessels in the head that have been pinched due to a high level of adrenaline are finally able to relax. The vessels quickly fill with blood, causing a headache.

When a migraine strikes on the weekend, plans with family and friends are often cancelled. Having to miss out on fun can sometimes cause depression. The depression further aggravates any existing headache and can also lead to more headaches. It's a vicious cycle, and it often-feels unfair that you have to suffer through it.

If you are dealing with stress-induced head pain, you're not alone. There are many ways to combat the stress in your life. Your doctor can help you find stress management or time management courses. Relaxation techniques can also help. Different relaxation exercises are outlined in chapter 13. Lowering your amount of daily stress and keeping busy during less stressful times may also reduce the frequency of your stress-related headaches by moderating the release of chemicals within your brain.

Sleep

In times of stress, sleeping habits are usually disturbed. Too little sleep can trigger a headache. But a severe tension headache or migraine can also make it impossible to sleep. This cycle can make the existing head pain worse and increase the frequency of headache and migraine attacks. In contrast, too much sleep can also trigger a headache. This may be one reason some people have headaches on the weekend: They sleep late to compensate for a lack of sleep during the week.

Developing a sleep schedule is the best way to avoid sleep triggered headaches. If you feel that too little or too much sleep is a trigger for you, set a routine for yourself. Try to go to bed about the same time each night and get up at the same time each morning. Avoid naps and oversleeping, if possible. Although it may be tempting to sleep in or nap on a weekend, try to avoid it if you are headache prone. Developing regular sleeping habits can even keep your chronic headaches or migraines in check. Sleep is a weapon that you can use against your head pain.

Physical Activity

Physical activity is another complicated trigger. Many times, exercise or strenuous exertion can relieve a headache. It is also a great way to relieve stress. In some people, though, exercise causes pain.

Some researchers think that conditions surrounding physical activity may contribute to triggering a migraine or headache. If exercise is done outdoors, the weather, atmospheric conditions, and altitude may stimulate a headache. The condition of the person performing the exercise may also contribute. If you play a game of soccer and didn't sleep well the night before, or have a very low carbohydrate level when you're playing, your chances of getting a headache increase.

You may not have control over some of these conditions around you, but pinpointing the exact triggers that cause your headaches may help you to avoid them.

Finding Help for Your Pain

For many years, headaches and migraine pain were not taken seriously. Doctors devoted very little time to researching head pain. Headaches were thought to be psychological problems and that there was not any real physical pain involved. In the 1700s, people thought that headaches were a result of repressed anger. In the 1800s many people who experienced recurring headaches were labelled as "troubled" and placed in mental asylums.

The theory that headaches were a psychological disease endured until the latter part of the twentieth century. Up until then, migraine sufferers were thought to exhibit certain personality traits. These people were said to be neurotic, compulsive, obsessive, rigid, and repressing a great deal of hostility. Scientific research was conducted that has proven that this is, of course, not the case. People who suffer from headaches and migraines have personalities no different than anyone else.

Nobody knows your pain like you do. In fact, you may be your own best doctor, since you have the time and incentive to study your case in great detail. It's up to you to communicate your headache problems to your doctor. Then the two of you can map out the best treatment options for your specific pain.

69

Medical Practitioners

Today there are a variety of different doctors and specialists who are working on treatments for headaches and migraines. The most important step you can take is to find a doctor with whom you feel comfortable. Unfortunately, some doctors still may believe that headache pain is really "all in your head." If you find yourself with a doctor like this, try to state exactly what you are feeling. Insist upon treatment you feel is right for you. If you think your doctor isn't taking you seriously, find a different doctor.

Your Primary Care Physician

Many medical insurance companies will have you or your family pick one doctor from whom you receive most of your medical care. This doctor is known as your primary care physician. A primary care physician is often a family doctor or general practitioner. This means that he or she is able to diagnose and treat many different sicknesses or injuries. A primary care physician is also a doctor who is able to refer you to doctors who treat specific conditions.

If your headaches or migraines seem fairly typical, or don't indicate a serious underlying disease, your primary care physician should be able to treat them. If you feel the diagnosis is wrong or that you want a second opinion, be sure to ask.

Specialists

If your headaches are not relieved by standard treatments, your primary care physician may refer you to a specialist. A specialist is a doctor who has studied and trained

70

specifically in the diseases or injuries of a particular part of the body. A specialist may be better able to pinpoint the causes of your pain. He or she may also be aware of the more obscure causes of pain—ideas that your general practitioner may not know as well as the specialist.

If standard treatments and medications do not help, your primary care physician may ask that you see a neurologist. A neurologist specializes in diseases and disorders of the central nervous system. This includes your brain, spinal cord, nerves, and muscles with which the nerves interact. Your primary care physician may also ask that you see a neurologist if he or she suspects something serious is causing your headaches. If something in your nervous system is not performing as it should, the neurologist will be able to detect that. Hopefully, he or she will also be able to diagnose and alleviate your headaches.

A physical therapist may also be called upon to treat your headaches. A physical therapist is a specialist who works to return your muscles to health after extensive injury or disease. A physical therapist may be able to alleviate some headaches by treating the muscles that aggravate chronic headaches. Tight neck and shoulder muscles often contribute to headaches and migraines.

Your primary care physician may also think that a psychologist or a psychiatrist may be able to help your headaches. A psychologist is a specialist who studies the mind and the behavior of people. A psychiatrist also studies the behavior of people, but unlike a psychologist, he or she also has a medical degree. This means that the psychiatrist can prescribe medication if it is needed.

If you are under a lot of stress or are experiencing many problems, this could contribute to your headaches. A psychologist can teach you ways to handle stress and prevent headaches. A psychiatrist can also teach you those things, but he or she is also able to diagnose emotional conditions such as depression. Medication may be needed to treat a problem and may give relief of headaches at the same time.

People who have been suffering from migraines or other headaches that seem uncontrollable often seek help from a headache specialist. A headache specialist is a doctor who concentrates only on treating people with headaches. Generally a headache specialist is contacted when all other treatments have been tried and have failed. The causes and treatments of headaches are not very specific, and they vary from person to person. New information and medicines are becoming available every day. Headache specialists are more aware of the newest advances in headache treatments. They also have more experience dealing with very difficult headache cases.

Alternative Practitioners

Any type of treatment outside of conventional medicine in the United States is considered alternative medicine. Some alternative medicines are standard treatments in other countries. Most forms of alternative medicines require that practitioners be licensed. To ensure that you are working with a reputable alternative medical practitioner, be sure to get a reference from your doctor.

A massage therapist is an example of an alternative medicine practitioner who works on the muscles of your body. His or her job is to manipulate different muscles in the body to reduce pain and muscle tightness that could lead to head pain. Massage therapists can also help to improve flexibility and bring about a greater range of motion in your joints. Massage therapy has been proven to reduce the pain of headaches and to prevent future headaches from occurring.

Acupuncture is another form of alternative medicine. An acupuncturist is a person who practices the traditional Chinese medicine therapy that involves the placement of thin needles in very specific places on the body. The placement of these needles is designed to regulate body systems and stimulate health within the body. Many people have turned to acupuncture as a way to combat their migraines and other chronic headaches.

A chiropractor is considered to be an alternative practitioner by some people and a mainstream doctor by others. Chiropractors attend chiropractic schools instead of traditional medical schools. Chiropractic medicine follows the theory that different disorders in the body result from the misalignment of bones and their corresponding nerves. Chiropractors adjust different body structures, such as the spinal column, to help heal a variety of disorders. Chiropractic medicine has given some people profound relief from their head pain.

Medical History

To make a proper diagnosis, your doctor will need to know all about your medical history. Many questions are easy; others may make you feel uncomfortable. It is important that you are very honest in answering all the questions. Information is key for your doctor to help treat your headaches.

Questionnaire

It may be helpful to answer as many of the following questions as you can before your doctor's appointment. This will give you more time to think about and provide more complete answers. Your doctor may ask you some of the following questions:

- What is your medical history? Previous illnesses, injuries, and allergies are all important factors to know when making a diagnosis.

- What is your family's medical history? Migraines and other diseases that may cause headaches often run in families.

- Are you taking any medications? The doctor will need to know about any prescribed medications or other drugs that you may be using.

- Do you use caffeine or alcohol, and do you smoke?

- What is your diet like?

- How are you sleeping? Any significant changes in your sleeping habits can indicate different problems to a doctor.

- How is your overall health? Problems in your life, such as a divorce or the death of a loved one, as

74

well as constant strains, such as schoolwork, may contribute to headaches.

Your doctor will also ask specifically about your headaches:

➷ When did you first start having headaches?

➷ How painful were those headaches on a scale of one to five?

➷ How do your headaches now compare with your first headaches?

➷ How often do you get headaches?

➷ Is the pain worse on one side of your head then the other?

➷ Are you able to continue your daily routines while you have a headache?

➷ Does the pain worsen with activity?

➷ Do you feel sick or feel like vomiting during a headache?

➷ Do lights or noises bother you more than usual during a headache?

➷ Is there a time of day when you get headaches more often?

➷ Are there any activities that seem to bring about a headache?

➥ Which of the following words best describe your headaches: Splitting, pounding, piercing, blinding, throbbing, stabbing, or aching?

➥ If you are female, do you get headaches before, during, or after your period?

➥ Have you found any treatments that seem to work at least some of the time?

➥ Are you concerned that your headaches might be a serious condition?

Headache Diary

A headache diary can be a very valuable tool in getting help for your migraines and other headaches. Write down the date and the time each headache starts in a notebook or on a piece of paper. How long did the headache last? Did it return? Draw a simple picture of a head. Circle the location of the pain. Try to use descriptive words to explain the pain. For example, was it a constant, dull ache or a piercing pain? Do this for about two to three months.

It is also helpful to keep your food record in your headache diary. Write down what you eat, including all meals, snacks, and beverages. Make sure to include any caffeine and medications that you are taking.

You should also include what you think caused the headache in your headache diary. Were you out jogging or studying for a test? Did you do anything or take any medications that stopped the headache? Keep track of how many days of school or work you had to miss because of headaches. Note any time that a headache interferes with your daily activities. Write down the time you go to bed and the time you get up. If you have problems sleeping or wake frequently during the night, you need to indicate that too.

Once you have a careful record, a cause for your headaches or migraines may become apparent. Bring your headache diary with you to any doctor's appointments. The information in your diary can help your doctor treat your specific pain. A headache diary can also be effective in helping to convince any skeptical doctors that your pain is real and is a serious problem.

Headache Clinics

If you and your primary care physician have tried everything to manage your head pain and nothing has really worked, he or she may refer you to a headache clinic. This is a specialized clinic that works to manage the pain of headache sufferers. If you feel that your headaches haven't improved with traditional medicine, it is okay to ask your primary care physician for a referral to a headache clinic.

A headache clinic may either be inpatient or outpatient. At an inpatient clinic, people who are seeking treatment stay overnight at the facility for the length of their treatment. Inpatient clinics often only handle people who are in excruciating pain and incapable of handling their daily lives. Inpatient clinics are staffed and equipped to help people who need intensive medical treatment.

Outpatient clinics treat people on an appointment basis. An outpatient clinic may include visits to different

77

doctors' offices or an arranged program in one clinic, called a day hospital.

A headache clinic often uses the multi-disciplinary approach to treatment. This means that there are many different specialists who will examine you. All the doctors at a headache clinic have focused their specialties on the treatment of headaches. You may be treated by physicians, neurologists, psychologists, psychiatrists, and physical therapists.

Your initial visits to any headache clinic will include different medical tests to rule out any underlying disease. Your past medical records will be evaluated. Then a psychologist will visit with you. The psychologist will seek a very thorough history of your headaches. Your emotional state will be discussed. The psychologist will be looking for any factors in your life that may bring about headaches or worsen existing headaches. The psychologist will also be looking for how much control over your headaches you can realistically expect to have.

Your team of physicians will then move forward with your treatment. This may include conventional medicine and physical therapy. Your treatment may also include stress-management courses or relaxation techniques.

To find a headache clinic, first consult your primary care physician. Several of the organizations listed in the appendix will also be able to give references. University hospitals are another good source of information about creditable specialists and headache clinics.

Visit a clinic before deciding whether this approach to headache pain management is good for you. Ask questions about the doctors and the success they have had in treating pain similar to yours. You will want to find out how much relief they can expect to give you. One of the most important factors you should look for in your care is that the doctors genuinely care about you and have an interest in your problem. Take the time to find the doctor and the treatment that is right for you.

At the Doctor's Office

Once you have chosen a doctor, it is important to prepare for your first visit. Your initial visit will be a time for you and your doctor to get to know each other. This is the time to present your headache diary and discuss your prepared questionnaire. The more information you can give the doctor about your headaches, the better he or she will be able to understand your needs. Then the two of you can begin to formulate a treatment.

Your first visit with any doctor may include questions that seem unrelated to your head pain. You may be given a short test. The doctor isn't trying to find out how smart you are. He or she wants an indication of how your brain is functioning. If you seem very confused and unable to answer simple questions, that may give the doctor a sign that something in your brain isn't working right.

Many people find that they need more than one visit to their doctor before they find the relief they need. It can take a while to try different medications or therapy. Most doctors like to try a therapy for at least three to four weeks before deciding if it is working for you or not. This takes a great deal of patience on your part. Keep writing in your headache diary. Only you can explain exactly what you feel and want. You are the key to helping your doctor treat you in the best possible way.

80

Physical Exam

After talking with your doctor, he or she will decide whether to run further tests. There is no specific test or exam, like there is for other diseases, that can positively diagnose a migraine condition. For example, a simple blood test can determine whether a person has AIDS. But there is no such test for migraines.

There is also no set way of determining what is causing your headaches. It can be very complicated to understand why you have headaches. Some people never really know. Tests will also help the doctor determine the best course of treatment for you.

The doctor may ask you to put on an examining gown. You will then be given a physical exam to see if there are any obvious problems that may be causing your headaches. The doctor will examine your eyes, ears, and throat. Your jaw and mouth may be examined for any problems. The doctor may look for any possible signs of a sinus infection. A stethoscope will be used to listen to your heart. Your skin may also be checked for any abnormalities.

The doctor may give you a motor exam. During this test, the doctor examines your control over your body, your coordination, and your mobility. Any problem with the functioning of your brain and nervous system may show up in this test. You may be asked to press against resistance and walk around the room. The doctor may also want you to flex your muscles and touch your finger to your nose.

Next, the doctor may test some of your senses. You may be asked to close your eyes and try to identify different objects that are placed in your hands. The doctor may

81

lightly prick your skin in different places on your body to see if your nerves can feel it. You may also be asked to wiggle your toes.

Depending on what the doctor discovers during your physical exam, and how bad your headaches are, the doctor may order more tests. These tests may include X rays, blood tests, and head scans. If you have complained of any symptoms that are out of the ordinary, your doctor will probably test for the causes of these too. These symptoms may include any dizziness, tingling, weakness, numbness, and clumsiness or any unusual coordination problems.

CAT (CT) Scan

CAT scan stands for computerized axial tomography. A CAT scan is also called a CT scan. It is a special kind of X ray that takes pictures of your brain. It is a painless procedure that requires you to lie on a platform for several minutes while a machine rotates around your head, taking pictures. Doctors are able to read the pictures and tell what is happening inside your skull. Hemorrhages, tumors, and strokes can all be detected by a CAT scan. Generally, however, most people with migraines have nothing unusual show up on their CAT scans.

Magnetic Resonance Imaging (MRI)

An MRI, or magnetic resonance imaging, is another kind of X ray. An MRI can take pictures of all parts of your body. Hemorrhages, tumors, and strokes can all be detected by an MRI. Unlike the CAT scan, however, an MRI can tell if there is decreased blood flow in different areas. Many people with migraines often show decreased blood flows in certain parts of their brains. An MRI can also detect abnormal blood vessels.

An MRI is a painless procedure. A dye may be injected into your blood vessels to show greater contrast between normal brain tissues and any abnormalities. Then you lie down in a chamber-like machine. Some people, particularly those who are claustrophobic, or have a fear of enclosed spaces, request a calming medication before the test. While you are lying in the chamber you are able to talk to the MRI technician or listen to a radio. Some people fall asleep during their MRI.

Electroencephalogram (EEG)

An electroencephalogram, or EEG, studies brain wave patterns. The electrical patterns are converted by a machine and then recorded on paper. It is a painless exam during which many people fall asleep. During the exam, electrodes are attached to your scalp and on different places on your body. You will sit in a chair or lie down on an examining table while the machine is working. Usually an EEG will show normal brain wave patterns between migraine attacks. Abnormal results are quite common during an actual migraine episode.

Angiography

If your doctor feels that you may have a weak or abnormal blood vessel, he or she will do a angiography. An abnormal blood vessel could be the cause of headaches. A doctor may think you have an abnormal blood vessel from the questions you answered, the physical exam, or from an MRI.

An angiography allows a doctor to examine blood vessels without having to perform surgery. The doctor inserts a tiny tube into a vein in your inner thigh. This vein is an arterial vein that leads to the heart and then to the brain. A harmless dye is then inserted into the tube. The dye travels through the vein, allowing doctors to get a better X ray of heart and brain activity.

There is a little bit of pain involved in an angiography, but most people don't think it's too bad. The entire procedure usually lasts about an hour.

Lumbar Puncture

A lumbar puncture is also known as a spinal tap. During this procedure, a needle is inserted into your lower back area. The needle withdraws a bit of the fluid from the spinal column that surrounds the spinal cord and the brain. The withdrawn fluid is tested. This fluid can tell the doctor a lot about any abnormalities within the brain. Infections, meningitis, hemorrhages, and other inflammatory disorders can be detected through a lumbar puncture.

This test can be painful. A good doctor, however, should be able to perform the procedure with little pain. A lumbar puncture usually rules out conditions for a person suffering from a migraine rather than explaining what is causing the headache. Often, the fluid is normal between headache attacks and abnormal during an attack.

Other Tests

Your sinuses may be x-rayed to rule out blocked sinus passages or infection. Your doctor may request a blood or urine sample from you to explore other possibilities for your headaches. He or she may want to rule out diabetes, anemia, thyroid dysfunction, and other disorders as causes of the head pain. Specialists may order a completely different set of these tests from what your primary care physician ordered.

First-Line and Second-Line Medications

For many centuries, people have desperately searched for a way to get rid of their headaches. They used the most modern medicines, tools, and technology that were available to them at that time. To relieve headache pain during the Stone Age, people would cut away at their skulls with pieces of sharp rock. During the first century, headache sufferers placed a hot iron against their foreheads. In the British Isles around the ninth century, headache sufferers drank a headache remedy that was a combination of cow brain, goat dung, and elderseed dissolved in vinegar.

Bloodletting was also a popular headache treatment of the past. This method used leeches which attached themselves to a patient's skin and sucked blood out of the person's body. It was thought that whatever was causing the headaches would drain out of the body with the blood. Bloodletting was used by doctors as standard treatment for many years. Thankfully, today we have easier and more effective ways of stopping pain from migraines and other headaches.

For the past century, the traditional way of fighting head pain has been through medications. For many years, migraine and other headache sufferers had to make do with only a few medicines that seemed to work only half the time. Now there are a variety of drugs that have been

86

proven to relieve the pain of migraines and other headaches. First-line medications are drugs that doctors generally like to try first. These medications are effective, but they are not the strongest drugs available. The goal of any treatment is for you to be taking the least amount of medication to control your pain. Doctors usually like to start out with a lower dose to see if that works before asking you to try a higher dose or a stronger medication.

This chapter outlines some of the medications that stop a headache in progress. Chapter 11 discusses medications that act to prevent headaches before they start.

The medications discussed in this chapter are generally available in two different types: prescription and over-the-counter. Over-the-counter medications are medicines that anyone can buy at most grocery or drug stores. There is a wide selection of over-the-counter medications from which to choose. You may have to try several different kinds before finding one that works for you. Tension headaches usually respond very well to over-the-counter medications, but talk to your doctor before trying any medications..

Prescription-strength drugs are medications that must be prescribed by a doctor. If your doctor feels that you need stronger medication, he or she will give you a written prescription to be filled at a pharmacy. Generally, people who suffer from migraines need the extra strength of a prescription medication.

Rebound Headaches

While headache medications can help to ease pain, they actually cause headaches in some cases. Rebound headaches are headaches that are caused by the medications that are supposed to stop head pain.

Rebound headaches occur when medications are taken too frequently. When too much medication enters your body, it begins to interfere with the brain's pain control system. The brain needs more and more of the drug, and if it doesn't get it, your head may begin to hurt. Many over-the-counter medications and some prescription drugs can cause rebound headaches. Check dosage guidelines and only take the prescribed amount to prevent these headaches.

Before taking any medications, talk to your doctor or pharmacist. Medications work differently in each person. You may be sensitive, or even allergic, to a particular medication. A doctor or pharmacist can discuss possible side effects with you. They can also recommend medications that might be better suited for you. It may take several months of trying different medications before you and your doctor find the one that works best for you.

Abortive Medications

If you were cooking dinner on the stove and one of the pans caught fire, you would most likely reach for the fire extinguisher at the first spark. If you didn't put out the flames right away, the fire would quickly get out of control. The fire could even spread to other parts of the house.

You can think of treating your headaches in much the same way. You should try to extinguish the pain immediately, before it gets worse or spreads to other parts of your body.

Abortive medications are drugs that are taken to stop a headache that has already started. To have maximum effect, abortive medications should be taken at the very first sign that a migraine or headache is about to strike. Any medication that is taken in pill form must first pass through your digestive system and into your bloodstream before you feel relief. This process can take anywhere from twenty to sixty minutes. That's why it is best to take the medication immediately.

If nausea is a problem for you during your headache and you wait to take a medication, the medication may not stay in your stomach long enough to work because it may be vomited out. Taking medication at any point, however, is better than taking none at all.

Abortive medications are available in both prescription and over-the-counter varieties. Generally, these medications are in pill form and are meant to be swallowed. Some abortive medications are available in an injectable, or shot, form. These medications work faster than pills because they are injected right into the bloodstream. You also don't have to worry about worsening any nausea, since no medication passes through the stomach. Injectable medications still do, however, need to be taken at the first sign of a headache.

Other abortive medications are also available as suppositories. A suppository is a capsule that is inserted into your rectum. Medicine contained in a suppository is absorbed by the bloodstream very quickly. A suppository is also an effective and fast-acting treatment.

Abortive medications work best in people who only occasionally experience headaches. If you have a migraine or other type of headache two or three times a week, talk to your doctor about medicine therapy for your migraines or other headaches. Chapter 11 outlines those types of medications.

Unfortunately, migraines cannot be cured, but the pain can often be relieved with medication. There is a wide range of medications to choose from to fit your specific needs. Sometimes a severe tension headache and a mild migraine have many of the same symptoms. For this reason, some medication designed specifically for a migraine may also work for a severe tension headache.

Aspirin

Aspirin has long been the medication most people reach for when they have a headache. For most tension headaches and other minor head pain, aspirin is very effective.

Aspirin's impact on migraines varies. Aspirin can work well if taken at the very onset of a mild migraine. But it will probably have no pain-relieving effect on more intense migraines or migraines that are already full blown.

Aspirin is an analgesic, or pain reliever. It works in several ways to relieve pain. Aspirin blocks and reduces inflammation or swelling of tissues and blood vessels. Chemicals found naturally in the body, called prostaglandins, are partly responsible for this swelling. Many researchers believe that a swelling of blood vessels in the head can contribute to a headache. Aspirin makes it very difficult for the body to produce prostaglandins.

Some researchers now believe that fluctuating levels of serotonin may be responsible for migraines and other headaches. Aspirin plays a part in this by affecting platelets, or the part of the blood that helps in clotting. When platelets stick together, they release the chemical serotonin. Aspirin prevents platelets from sticking together and affecting the serotonin levels in the body.

Some people experience some stomach upset when taking aspirin. If nausea or vomiting is already a problem with a migraine, then it is probably best to stay away from aspirin. With a tension headache, a buffered aspirin may help to ward off any stomach problems.

Bayer is one brand of aspirin. Anacin is another over-the-counter brand that combines aspirin with caffeine. Studies have shown that small amounts of caffeine may enhance the pain-relieving properties in certain medications.

Taking too much aspirin can bring about serious stomach ailments and other problems. Children and adolescents should not take aspirin without first checking with a doctor, especially if they feel that they may have the flu. In certain cases, aspirin can be very harmful to children.

Acetaminophen
Many people take acetaminophen for their headaches, and it is particularly effective on tension headaches. It does not seem to work as well, however, on severe headaches or migraines. Acetaminophen has less side effects than aspirin, and is gentler on the stomach. One popular over-the-counter brand is Tylenol.

In some cases, taking caffeine with acetaminophen can make it work better. Aspirin-Free Excedrin is an over-the-counter medication that contains acetaminophen plus caffeine. The caffeine may, however, cause nervousness or insomnia in some people. And taking too much Aspirin-Free Excedrin may cause rebound headaches.

Extra Strength Excedrin

Extra Strength Excedrin is the brand name for a medication that is effective against migraines. It has recently been recognized by the Food and Drug Administration (FDA) as an accepted over-the-counter remedy for migraines. Extra Strength Excedrin is a combination of acetaminophen, aspirin, and caffeine. Taken at the very beginning of a migraine, Extra Strength Excedrin may relieve the throbbing pain. It can be used at any time for other headaches, and it is considered one of the most effective over-the-counter medicines available for tension headaches.

Due to the high dose of caffeine in Extra Strength Excedrin, taking too much may result in rebound headaches. The caffeine may also cause anxiety and the aspirin can cause nausea or heartburn. Sufferers who can't handle the side effects of the aspirin in Extra Strength Excedrin may find relief with the aspirin-free version of this medication.

Ibuprofen

Ibuprofen is an anti-inflammatory drug that may help stop the swelling of blood vessels in your head. Ibuprofen works by blocking certain body chemicals, such as prostaglandins, that cause inflammation. Some researchers believe that when the blood vessels swell, they pinch against nerves. This can be causing the pain. By stopping the swelling, anti-inflammatory drugs help reduce the pain of a headache.

Ibuprofen is commonly sold as the over-the-counter drug Advil or in prescription strength as Motrin. Motrin is also available in non-prescription strength. Ibuprofen may at times be effective against mild migraines, but you may need to try the prescription strength of Motrin to experience any relief. Ibuprofen seems to work better than acetaminophen in treating tension and other headaches.

Side effects with ibuprofen are minimal. It is one of the easiest drugs on the stomach; there is usually no upset. And ibuprofen does not normally cause rebound headaches. However, if you find yourself taking a large amount of ibuprofen and exceeding the recommended dosage, call your doctor. An excess of ibuprofen can harm your liver and kidneys, and you may need another kind of medication for your pain.

Naproxen Sodium

If ibuprofen isn't helpful to your headaches, you may experience more relief from naproxen sodium. Naproxen sodium is a drug that can be used for many types of headaches, but works particularly well on treating headaches that are triggered by menstruation. It is sold without a prescription under the brand name Aleve and with a prescription as Anaprox. Naproxen sodium is sometimes used as a preventative medication against mild migraines. One advantage to using Aleve is that it lasts longer than other pain medications, so you don't have to take it as frequently.

There may be stomach upset when taking naproxen sodium. Eating food or taking an antacid with the pill may help to prevent this. Naproxen sodium isn't meant to be taken daily for a long period of time.

Second-Line Medications

Second-line medications are abortive headache treatments that doctors usually try after your headaches haven't responded to lower-strength medications. Some of the second-line medications are so strong that they can be addictive or have some very unpleasant side effects. For this reason, your doctor will want to see if the first-line medications work on your migraines or other headaches.

Second-line medications are only available by prescription. Your doctor will monitor you to see how well your headaches react to these medications. Your doctor will also want to know about any side effects that you experience.

There are many different drugs and combinations of those drugs that are being researched and tested all the time. The medications listed here are a few that have been found to be safe and effective. Your doctor will work with you to determine which medications will work best for you.

Norgesic Forte

Norgesic Forte is a brand name for a medication that is effective for both tension headaches and mild migraines. Norgesic Forte is a combination of aspirin, caffeine, and a muscle relaxant. Norgesic Forte is one of the strongest, nonaddictive abortive medications.

Fatigue and nausea are common side effects of Norgesic Forte. You may also feel lightheaded and have blurred vision.

Midrin

Midrin is the brand name for an abortive prescription medication. It contains a vasoconstrictor (an ingredient

94

that reduces the swelling of blood vessels), a sedative (to relax muscles), and acetaminophen. Midrin has been proven to be very effective against even the most intense migraines. It can also be used for severe tension headaches.

Midrin can cause sleepiness. You may also feel slightly sick to your stomach or lightheaded from taking Midrin.

Sumatriptan/Imitrex

Sumatriptan is an abortive drug that is most commonly sold under the brand name Imitrex. It is used to stop a migraine in progress. It is considered to be the most effective anti-migraine medication currently available.

Sumatriptan can be taken either by injection or in pill form. It can stop a headache that is already three or four hours into its cycle, although taking it as early as possible works best. The injectable form seems to work better, stopping headaches about 80 percent of the time. The shot also works more rapidly, within ten minutes of injection, and in lower doses than the tablets. Sumatriptan tablets usually reduce migraine pain within two to four hours after taking the pills. The tablets may also relieve the nausea and inability to withstand bright lights that sometimes come with a migraine. But sumatriptan can cause side effects in some people. The most commonly reported ones are sleepiness, a tingling sensation, discomfort in the nose, and dizziness.

Ergotamines

Ergotamines are one of the most commonly used drugs for both classic and common migraines. This class of drugs is derived from a fungus, and works by keeping the blood vessels in your head from swelling and pressing on nerves. Ergotamines, however, only seem to work during the initial stages of a migraine. If your head is already pounding, this medication probably won't help. Ergotamines are recommended for people who have few, but severe, migraine attacks.

Ergotamines are available as pills, shots, or suppositories. Nausea and vomiting are common side effects of ergot alkaloids. Doctors will often prescribe an anti-nausea drug to combat this. Ergotamines are not meant to be taken often, and people with heart, liver, or kidney problems should not use them. Ergotamines can cause serious side effects if too many are taken, including hallucinations. They can also be addictive.

Wigraine and Cafergot are two effective prescription drugs against migraines that both contain ergotamine. They also have high levels of caffeine. The caffeine can cause sleeplessness and listlessness in some people. Other ergot alkaloids include Ergomar, Ergostat, and Dihydroergotamine (DHE).

Butalbital Compounds

Butalbital is made from barbiturates. Barbiturates are sedatives that depress the central nervous system. A butalbital compound combines butalbital with aspirin, acetaminophen, or other medications.

The major concern with taking butalbital compounds is the high potential for addiction. The FDA has approved butalbital compounds for use against tension headaches. They are also prescribed for people who have mild, infrequent migraines. In general, butalbital compounds are prescribed when other medications have failed. They are meant to be taken once a week or less. The generic brands of butalbital compounds do not seem to work as effectively as the brand names.

Fiorinal is the most effective of the butalbital compounds. Common side effects are fatigue, nausea, and lightheadedness. People who take a higher dose than was prescribed of Fiorinal may get a high from it that could lead to addiction.

Fioricet and Esgic are examples of other butalbital compounds. They differ from Fiorinal in that they contain acetaminophen instead of aspirin. Fioricet and Esgic can cause fatigue, nervousness, and a lightheaded feeling. They rarely cause nausea.

Cluster Headache Treatments

As mentioned earlier, a cluster headache is one kind of migraine that got its name from its tendency to occur in groups, or clusters, over a few days to even a few weeks or months. Doctors treat all cluster headaches the same, whether they occur frequently or only once in a while. Any medication for cluster headaches must be fast-acting, since the pain is excruciating. Even though the average length of a cluster headache is less than one hour, it can be a debilitating and miserable experience.

Oxygen

Inhaling pure oxygen is one of the most effective treatments for cluster headaches. There are no side effects and it can be done in combination with other medications.

Most cluster headache sufferers rent an oxygen tank and mask. At the first sign of an attack, the person tries to sit comfortably and lean slightly forward while inhaling from the mask. The oxygen can be used for up to two hours in one day. Most cluster sufferers only need to use the oxygen for about fifteen or twenty minutes until the pain starts to lessen.

Ergotamines

Ergotamines are somewhat effective in treating cluster headaches, and cluster headache sufferers do not seem to get the rebound headaches that people sometimes have when they are taking ergotamines for migraines.

Ergotamines should not be taken frequently, or by people with heart, liver, or kidney problems. Younger people who suffer from cluster headaches may have more success with ergotamines than older people. Caution must be used when taking ergotamines because of their serious side effects and addictive properties.

Cafergot is one prescription drug containing ergotamine and caffeine. It is available in both pill and suppository form. Ergostat is another abortive cluster headache medication with ergotamine that is available.

DHE, or dihydroergotamine, is an effective ergotamine that is available as a pill, injection, or nasal spray. The injection is most effective, but many people do not want to give themselves a shot in the middle of an intense cluster headache. DHE has many side effects, including nausea, leg cramps, a burning sensation around the injection area, diarrhea, tightness in the throat or chest, and a flushed and burning feeling in the head. These effects, however, usually subside within a day. Intravenous DHE is another form of this very powerful drug that needs to be monitored while given. Sometimes this drug can also be administered in a doctor's office.

Sumatriptan/Imitrex

Sumatriptan, or Imitrex, is sold in both pill and injectable form. It is better at stopping a migraine than a cluster headache, but it can sometimes work with cluster headaches. The sumatriptan pills usually don't have enough time to act on a cluster headache. But if a sufferer is willing to give himself an injection, sumatriptan will usually stop the pain.

There are minimal side effects with sumatriptan. There is usually some burning pain at the site where the shot was given, but rubbing ice on the skin before giving the shot helps to prevent this pain. Other side effects can include a tingling sensation, heat flashes, dizziness, and a feeling of weakness. Most of the side effects of sumatriptan disappear quickly.

Emergency Room Treatment

If your head pain becomes absolutely unbearable, and none of the first- or second-line abortive medications work for you, it may be time for a trip to the emergency room. Going to the hospital is never easy. If you haven't had any trauma to the head and have no other symptoms other than a headache, you may have to wait for treatment.

There is also the problem of insurance to consider when visiting the emergency room. Many insurance companies

99

won't pay for the trip unless you are in a life-threatening situation, and insurance companies do not consider a migraine to be life threatening. Be sure to try to contact your doctor first. Your doctor can tell you whether or not you should go to the emergency room. Most doctors have emergency telephone numbers so that he or she or a colleague can be reached for consultation at all times. By having a doctor's approval, most insurance companies will cover the emergency room visit. Without insurance, an emergency room visit can be very expensive.

A new problem has also surfaced for headache sufferers who go to the emergency room for treatment. Some doctors and nurses, unable to see any wounds, may think a person is faking symptoms to support a drug habit. The hospital staff often has a hard time distinguishing between those who are telling the truth and those who are lying about having a headache. This results in difficulty obtaining treatment.

One way to avoid problems in the emergency room is to see your doctor about preventative care. Chapter 11 outlines some of these treatments. If you find that you absolutely must go to the emergency room, bring along copies of your medical records. This can prove to the hospital staff that you are in fact being treated by a doctor for migraines or other headaches .

If you are having other symptoms that distinguishes *this* headache from other headaches you have experienced, a trip to the emergency room may be necessary. If you have a headache that is like a "thunderclap," a headache that gets worse with movement, any numbness in your arms or legs, or any head pain after a head injury, contact your doctor right away.

If you go to the emergency room with a migraine, you may receive an injection of a narcotic, such as Demerol, methadone, or morphine. You will probably also receive a tranquilizer, such as Valium. This combination of drugs will stop your pain and will probably make you sleepy. Usually, a fairly strong dose of drugs is needed to stop the pain. Anything that works to put you to sleep will be helpful, since sleep is the best weapon against a migraine.

The steroid drug cortisone is sometimes administered in the emergency room for a migraine. Sometimes cortisone is the only thing that will work for particularly bad head pain. Migraines triggered by menstruation, flying, and altitude all respond well to cortisone. The drug is given as an injection around certain nerves. Cortisone is such a powerful drug that a patient can only receive two shots per year. Cortisone is also commonly used to stop cluster headaches.

Cocaine nasal drops may also be used to stop a cluster headache. They are only used when everything else has failed. Cocaine nasal drops are highly addictive. If you have had any previous addictions to medications or other drugs, they can't be used. The small amount used does not usually produce a euphoric or high state, but if a high feeling is produced, then your dosage will need to be lowered. Cocaine nasal drops are used only in extreme cases to stop a cluster headache.

Preventing Head Pain

The average migraine sufferer has one to four attacks per month. People who suffer from chronic tension headaches have a headache at least fifteen times per month. It is very difficult to treat either type of headache with any over-the-counter medications. These sufferers have also usually tried every type of abortive medication they can find with no luck. They simply don't find any relief from medication taken after their headaches start.

Often people find that a great amount of pills need to be taken to relieve even a fraction of their pain. Taking so many pills is not good for your health. Many medications can easily lead to rebound headaches,. and taking a lot of medications can also be toxic to your body. Kidney failure is a common result of taking large amounts of certain drugs. Following dosage guidelines and only using the medications once in a while to prevent migraines and other headaches is a much healthier, and safer, treatment. Preventing your head pain is the better way to go than simply trying to cope with it.

Miranda

Miranda sat on her bed with her head in her hands. It felt like somebody was driving nails into her skull. The throbbing was unbearably intense and she knew

102

she would start throwing up soon. As she lay back on her bed in the dark, she could hear her friends driving away in their car. Her mom must have explained to them what was going on. Miranda was supposed to be going to the mall with her friends to buy shoes for the upcoming dance. But with this throbbing headache she couldn't even stand to keep her eyes open. This was her fourth headache this month. She worried every day about when the next one would strike. Miranda couldn't imagine not being able to go to the dance. But there was no way she could cope with a headache and be with her friends. When she felt better, Miranda knew she was going to have to call her doctor and find out if he could give her something to keep these headaches from coming back.

Prophylactic Medications

The best way to treat a migraine or any other severe headache is to stop it before it starts. A prophylactic, or preventative, is a medication that works to do just that—prevent pain from starting. Prophylactic drugs can be either over-the-counter or prescription medications. Often prophylactic drugs take a while to start working in the body. It is wise to give any preventative medication about four weeks to work before you try a different drug.

Your doctor can help you figure out if you would benefit from a prophylactic medication. It may take a while to discover the right prophylactic, and it takes a great deal of patience to find the right medication, but the end result is worth it. You will be headache-free.

Antidepressants

Antidepressants are medications that are commonly used to treat depression, but they are also very good in treating headaches. They are most often used to treat chronic tension headaches, but they can also be effective against migraines.

Some people who get a lot of headaches get depressed, too, but antidepressant drugs do not work on their headaches simply because they may be depressed. Antidepressant drugs have certain properties that affect the body's serotonin system.

A serotonin imbalance in your brain is thought by some doctors and researchers to be a cause of migraines and other headaches. Antidepressants work by balancing the levels of serotonin found in your brain. They may also prevent future headaches from occurring. Balancing the levels of serotonin may also lessen the severity and length of headaches that do sneak in.

Amitriptyline

Amitriptyline is an antidepressant sold under the brand name Elavil. It has been proven to be very effective against both migraines and chronic tension headaches. Amitriptyline works particularly well against combination migraine and tension headaches. It is the most commonly used and the most effective antidepressant for preventing tension head pain.

The downside to amitriptyline is its side effects. These can include significant weight gain, tranquilizing effects, and constipation. Lowering the dose can usually get rid of these symptoms. Dizziness, dry mouth, and anxiety may also occur when first taking amitriptyline, but these symptoms usually disappear after a while.

Fluoxetine

Fluoxetine is the antidepressant best known by its brand name, Prozac. Besides being one of the most popular antidepressants prescribed for people battling depression, it is also often used as a prophylactic against both migraines and chronic tension headaches. Fluoxetine is also very good at stopping combination headaches. It works by regulating the chemical serotonin, which is found in the brain.

Fluoxetine generally does not cause the weight gain, dry mouth, constipation, or fatigue that amitriptyline can. It can, however, cause anxiety, nausea, and sleeplessness.

Sometimes fluoxetine is combined with other medications to help ease the pain of a chronic tension headache. Fluoxetine can also help with the low levels of depression sometimes experienced by headache-prone people.

Doxepin

Doxepin is another antidepressant that can work as a prophylactic against headaches. It is sold in prescription form as Sinequan and Adapin. Doxepin is very similar to amitriptyline, and it works to prevent migraines and tension headaches. It also tackles the anxiety that many headache sufferers feel between headaches. Doxepin's side effects include fatigue and weight gain.

Protriptyline

Protriptyline is an antidepressant that is also used as a preventative medication for chronic tension headaches. It is sold as the prescription Vivactil. Protriptyline is not very effective on migraine pain, and it may not work as well as amitriptyline against chronic tension headaches. If you do not want to experience the weight gain and sedation that amitriptyline can cause, protriptyline may be the answer.

Some side effects of protriptyline include constipation, dry mouth, and dizziness. It may also cause insomnia, so it is best to take protriptyline in the morning.

Beta Blockers

Beta blockers have long been used to treat problems with the heart and circulatory system, including high blood pressure and coronary artery disease. In the 1960s, doctors accidentally discovered that beta blockers also work well in preventing migraines. The FDA approved the beta blocker propranolol to be used for migraine prevention in the 1970s. Nadolol is also an effective prophylactic.

Beta blockers are the second most common migraine preventative medication after amitriptyline. Beta blockers work by blocking the release of certain chemicals, including adrenaline, within your body. Too much adrenaline released in your body can contribute to migraines and other severe headaches.

Beta blockers lower your pulse and stabilize blood vessels by preventing them from dilating or expanding. Beta blockers also work to inhibit serotonin, which we already know plays a role in migraines.

All beta blockers are distributed by prescription. If you do begin taking beta blockers, you should never stop taking them abruptly. This can induce some serious health problems. Consult your doctor before you stop any medications he or she has prescribed for you.

Propranolol

The beta blocker propranolol, sold as the prescription Inderal, has long been used as a preventative for migraines. It has been used and researched extensively and is considered safe and effective. Propranolol can also be helpful with some severe tension headaches.

Although they are not very serious, numerous possible side effects are possible with propanolol use. These can include fatigue, upset stomach, diarrhea, depression, weight gain, and concentration problems.

Nadolol

The beta blocker nadolol, sold as Corgard, is as effective in preventing headaches as propranolol. Some people see relief of headache pain with nadolol when propranolol hasn't worked, and nadolol may cause fewer side effects than propranolol. One of the advantages of using nadolol is that it doesn't cause the intense fatigue that other medications do.

Nonsteroidal Anti-Inflammatory Drugs (NSAIDS)

Nonsteroidal anti-inflammatory drugs, or NSAIDs, are a class of drugs that work to prevent inflammation, or swelling, in the body. They are nonsteroidal, which means that they don't interfere with the body's growth and hormone systems. NSAIDS are available in both over-the-counter and prescription strengths and can help you with the pain of your migraines and headaches.

Typically, NSAIDS are not meant to be used on a long-term basis because they can be stored in the body, which can have devastating effects. You may experience stomach upset and liver and kidney damage from taking too many NSAIDS. If you have been using NSAIDS as an abortive medication, you can switch to a preventative one. A doctor will monitor you regularly to prevent the more harmful side effects.

NSAIDS have been proven to be very good against migraines brought on by menstruation. If one type of NSAID doesn't work, keep trying and don't give up hope. But remember: Never take any medications without first checking with your doctor.

Naproxen

Naproxen is the most frequently studied and widely prescribed NSAID for migraine prevention. Naproxen is sold in prescription strength as Naprosyn and Anaprox. It is sold in nonprescription strength as Aleve. Anaprox is effective as both a migraine and a tension abortive medication because it also contains sodium, which accelerates, or speeds up, the breakdown of medication in the body. Anaprox is often prescribed along with amitriptyline as a preventative.

Stomach upset and irritation are very common with naproxen. A doctor can prescribe something to soothe the stomach upset, or you can try an over-the-counter acid neutralizer or antacid. Eating food along with the medication can also help.

108

When naproxen is used as a daily preventative, there can be further side effects. Liver and kidney functions must be monitored to prevent any toxicity, or build-up. Skin rashes, fatigue, fluid retention, and ringing in the ears may also occur.

Fenoprofen

If your migraines and other headaches haven't found any relief from naproxen, fenoprofen may work, which is sold as the prescription medication Nalfon. People who experience chronic tension headaches may have more luck with fenoprofen than people who suffer from migraines.

If fenoprofen builds up in the body, it can become toxic. To prevent this, a doctor will need to monitor you closely. Other side effects can include stomach irritation, fatigue, and fluid retention.

Ketoprofen

Ketoprofen is an NSAID sold as the prescription or over-the-counter brand Orudis. Ketoprofen has been proven to be very good at preventing migraine headaches, but it does not work as well on preventing chronic tension headaches.

Side effects of ketoprofen are similar to those of other anti-inflammatory drugs. There may be some stomach upset, but taking the medication with food or with an antacid may help. If ketoprofen is used on a daily basis, a doctor must monitor liver and kidney functions closely because of the risk of build-up in the body. High amounts of ketoprofen can cause severe problems with these internal organs.

Calcium Channel Blockers

Calcium channel blockers are a group of prescription medications that were originally used to treat cardiovascular problems, or problems of the heart and circulatory system. Doctors then discovered that they were also good in preventing and treating migraines. Despite their name, calcium channel blockers have nothing to do with the body producing or using calcium.

Calcium channel blockers work by blocking calcium ions (molecules) from entering blood vessels when receptors for the migraine trigger chemicals are present. By interfering with these chemicals, the blood vessels don't go through the changes that can produce the pounding pain of a migraine. Calcium channel blockers are best known for their ability to prevent future migraines.

Calcium channel blockers are newer to the market than some of the other migraine preventatives, but they have been widely studied and are often just as effective as some of the beta blockers. Some doctors think calcium channel blockers are actually more useful against migraines with auras than are beta blockers.

Calcium channel blockers are also very helpful because they have very few side effects. Constipation, however, is one known side effect.

Verapamil

Verapamil is the most commonly used and most widely studied calcium channel blocker. It is also the most effective. It is sold by prescription as Isoptin, Calan, and

Veralan. When first taking verapamil, it may take up to six weeks until you notice any improvement in your headaches. But verapamil is safe when combined with other headache medications.

Most people experience very few side effects when using verapamil. Constipation is a common side effect. Swelling in the ankles and legs may also occur. On rare occasions, some people may experience rashes, insomnia, fatigue, and dizziness.

Cluster Headache Prophylactics

Most people who suffer from cluster headaches will need to take some type of preventative medication, since there is very little time for a drug to work to stop a cluster headache in progress. It is much easier to try to prevent the pain of a cluster headache before it even erupts.

Cluster headaches usually occur in cycles at certain times of the year, so medication is only needed at these times. Sometimes very few cluster headaches are experienced during the cycle. For these sufferers, breathing pure oxygen or another of the abortive medications may work. In general, however, most people who get cluster headaches want to be on a preventative because they don't even want to risk experiencing the pain.

Cortisone
Cortisone is a very fast-acting drug. It is usually given for one to two weeks at the beginning of a cluster cycle. This method of treatment prevents the first headache and gives other preventative drugs a chance to work. Cortisone may

be given again at the peak of a cluster cycle or when a headache is at its very worst. Cortisone may be given in pill form or as an injection.

There are many side effects of cortisone, which is why it is only used for a short period of time. When used so briefly, the side effects are minimal. Some people get nervous or moody when using cortisone. They may also have problems sleeping. Having an upset stomach is also a very common side effect.

Verapamil

Verapamil has been proven to work well against migraines and chronic tension headaches with few side effects. It can be combined with cortisone or lithium as a cluster headache preventative, or it can be used alone. For most cluster sufferers, verapamil becomes effective in only a few days.

Verapamil is a popular preventative because of its limited side effects. Many of the other preventatives cause weight gain and sedation. Verapamil does not. It may, however, cause allergic skin reactions, insomnia, and dizziness.

Lithium

Lithium is a prescription medication commonly used for a condition called bipolar disorder, and is also used by people who suffer from severe mood swings. Lithium has also been shown, however, to work on those who suffer from certain kinds of headaches.

Lithium is generally chosen for combatting cluster headaches if cortisone and verapamil have not brought relief. Lithium works better at stopping chronic cluster headaches, but it does stop episodic, or occasional, clusters as well.

Lithium is known for its many potential side effects. The doses given for cluster sufferers are so low that these side effects usually do not present problems. Your doctor will probably check your blood frequently to watch for any lithium build-up. Too much lithium can cause diarrhea, nausea, vomiting, tremors, and mood swings. Toxic levels of lithium can induce a coma. Even low doses of lithium can cause you to gain weight, become restless, and contract thyroid disease.

Lithium can cause excessive thirst in some users. If you drink lots of fluids because of this thirst, your kidneys may not be able to handle so much liquid if they are not working properly. Your doctor will monitor your kidney functions while taking lithium to ensure that they stay healthy.

Alternative Medicine

The best migraine treatment is the one that works for you. For some people, a mild medication taken at the onset of a headache can control all head pain. Other people may try every combination of medication available and worry that they may never find any relief. Many people also do not like the idea of having to take so many pills.

Luckily, there are other forms of treatment available for headaches besides medications. These treatments fall under the heading of alternative medicine. All that really means is that the treatments do not follow mainstream medical treatment found in the United States. Some of the treatments, such as acupuncture and yoga, have been practiced by other cultures for centuries.

Many of the alternative medical treatments are gaining widespread acceptance in the United States. Doctors are understanding the positive effects of different methods. Some medical insurance companies are even beginning to pay for some forms of alternative medicine, such as massage therapy and chiropractic.

There are many alternative medicine therapies available. This chapter will outline several that have been known to lessen head pain. Some therapies are even known to prevent future migraines and other headaches.

114

Not all forms of alternative medicine are strictly regulated. Some practitioners may not have studied their therapy with licensed professionals and may not have enough knowledge to properly administer treatment. To guard against this, always ask your doctor for a reference. University hospitals may also have a list of reputable alternative medicine practitioners.

As with any headache treatment, check with your doctor first. If the treatment makes your head pain worse, you should stop immediately. Don't be shy about asking doctors or other therapists about their treatments. They are there to help you in any way they can.

Yoga

Many people practice yoga on a daily basis as part of a fitness routine. But yoga can also provide relief from migraines and other headaches. Yoga is a system of exercises that helps the person achieve both physical and mental control. Its ultimate goal is a complete sense of physical and spiritual well-being.

Yoga originated more than five hundred years ago in India. It began as a Hindu philosophy and a way of living. Over the years, generations of people have modified yoga into many different philosophies and practices, but the basic goal of well-being has remained a constant. Even today, yoga is embraced by many as part of a healthy lifestyle.

The term "yoga" is an ancient word from the Indian and Hindu languages meaning "union." The union refers to a blend of your physical body with your inner being. It is a uniting of the body and the mind. Practitioners of yoga believe that the integration of the body and the mind will lead to good physical health, as well as happiness and a sense of mental peace.

Many people practice yoga. Athletes often try it to improve their energy and stamina. Businesspeople like it for its relaxing and calming effects. Other people try yoga for its abilities to tone and strengthen muscles, increase one's power of concentration, and improve memory.

A few of the basic forms of yoga are presented here. The system of breathing exercises is perhaps the most well-known for its ability to help some people with health problems. The breathing exercises cannot necessarily stop a full-blown migraine, but they have been able to reduce the pain of many headaches. Many people also believe that the exercise helps to prevent future migraines and other headaches. Yoga at the very least provides a form of relaxation that may help you find relief from your pain.

Asanas

Many of the yoga techniques incorporate exercises, stretching, and different body positions, or asanas. Asana literally means "steady pose." There are said to be more than 840,000 asanas. Some advanced asanas are meant to be held for a long period of time. During an asana, the goal is to remain both physically and mentally steady and comfortable.

The combination of stretching and exercising in asanas helps to improve your circulation, which helps to release tension and stress. The positions also help to strengthen and tone muscles. Healthy muscles are more resistant to injury. Asanas also improve your flexibility, particularly the flexibility of your back. Practitioners of asanas believe that because your spinal column is such a vital part of your central nervous system, the more flexible your back, the healthier you will be.

One of the twelve basic postures of asanas is the fish posture. Lie on a comfortable surface with your feet together. Place your arms next to your sides and lay your palms on the floor. Then slide your hands underneath your buttocks. Slowly begin to arch your spine. Tilt your head back so the top of your head touches the ground. Hold this position for a few seconds. Then slide your head back and lower your back to the ground. Relax in this position for a few moments.

The goal of the fish posture is to improve flexibility in your back and to ease tension. This posture also allows your chest to fully expand and provide easier breathing. The motion of lifting your chest with your arms tucked underneath releases pressure on nerves in your back. Practicing this exercise may help to prevent future head pain.

Meditation

Meditation is a type of yoga that is familiar to many people and is a form of contemplation and reflection. Its goal is fulfillment and happiness through awareness. Practitioners of meditation work to concentrate and focus their minds on even the smallest of details in their lives. They work to integrate the body, mind, and spirit by paying attention to every aspect of life.

True believers of meditation do not block or suppress thoughts and concerns. Instead, they strive to work through them. People who meditate want to solve their problems or learn to live with their stressors so they can be at peace with themselves.

Meditation involves the use of a mantra. A mantra is a sound, word, or phrase that you repeat to yourself over and over to increase concentration. Some people believe that a mantra should be a sound that has no meaning. If the mantra is just a sound and has no meaning, then you are better able to clear your mind of your usual thoughts.

There are many different ways to meditate. One simple form of meditation begins in a seated position with your eyes closed. Relax and breathe naturally. Begin repeating your mantra silently to yourself. Focus on your breathing. Slowly inhale and exhale. You may realize at different times that you are no longer thinking of your mantra. That's okay. Just try to forget all other thoughts and return to your mantra. Do not get frustrated or angry with yourself and force yourself to think of your mantra. Instead, gently bring yourself back to your mantra and remain relaxed.

Thinking about your mantra and focusing on your breathing should bring about a deeply relaxed state. Meditate in this way for no longer than twenty minutes. At the end of your meditation, slowly open your eyes. You may want to remain sitting for a few more minutes to allow your body to ease out of its totally relaxed state.

Meditation takes practice. Don't be discouraged if your mind wanders or if you feel fidgety the first few times. Keep trying, and soon you'll feel the benefits. Also, meditation should be practiced when you are feeling healthy. Then, when you have a headache, you may be able to slip into a meditative state that can relax you and ease your pain. Practicing a meditative state may also relieve daily stress and tension. This can help to reduce the number and frequency of your headaches. Lastly, falling asleep during meditation is okay. If you fall asleep, it means you have achieved your goal of relaxation. You are not meditating anymore if you fall asleep, but you are certainly relaxed.

Pranayama

"Prana" refers to energy, or what practitioners call the "vital air" within a person. "Yama" refers to the managing and routing of that energy. Pranayama is a type of yoga that applies the control of energy through breathing exercises. The belief of those who practice pranayama is that steady breathing can increase the amount of energy and vital air within oneself. Practitioners also believe that this increase results in better health.

To practice pranayama, it is important to wear loose-fitting, comfortable clothes. It is also important that you practice at a time when you are free from a cold or other ailment that could prevent you from breathing through your nose.

Pranayama implements what is known as "yoga breathing." This is a combination of breathing from the stomach and the chest. Mastering pranayama takes proper instruction and much practice. The basic version of pranayama follows:

1. Lie on a comfortable, flat surface; relax. Place one hand on your chest and the other on your stomach.

2. Inhale from your stomach. The hand on your stomach should rise while the one on your chest

remains still. Then inhale from your chest; your hand on your chest should also now rise. Once you cannot inhale anymore, begin to exhale. Exhale first from your chest and then from your stomach.

3. Breathe very slowly. If you feel dizzy, you are probably breathing too fast.

4. Once you feel comfortable with the yoga breathing, it is time to move to an upright position. Sit or stand with your spine fairly straight.

5. Now you will do the yoga breathing to a rhythm or pattern. For example, a 4-4-4-4 rhythm means to first inhale while mentally counting to four. Then hold your breath for four counts. Next, exhale for four counts. Hold your breath again for four counts. Then start the 4-4-4-4 rhythm all over again.

Pranayama should be practiced daily to achieve maximum results. The rhythm can be a very relaxing and calming exercise. It can help to ward off stress and tension, which in turn may fight off migraines and headaches.

Acupuncture

Acupuncture is a method of traditional Chinese medicine that uses the insertion of needles at precise points on the body to promote healing and general health. Acupuncture has been practiced for more than 2,000 years. It has been used not only in China but in other parts of Asia as well as around the world to treat many different disorders and diseases. Acupuncture is becoming increasingly popular in the United States as more people discover that neither drugs nor surgery are always needed to provide healing. There are also no side effects from acupuncture.

Traditional Chinese medicine is based on the theory of Yin and Yang. The belief is that good physical health comes from a balance between the principles of Yin and Yang. Yin represents negative, feminine principles. Yang represents positive, masculine principles. The Chinese have believed for thousands of years that for a person to achieve well-being, Yin and Yang need to be in balance. Yin Yang balance is the healthy state of the body.

The Chinese also believe that energy runs through the body and over its surface in specific channels. These channels are called meridians. The energy running through the meridians is known as Qi (pronounced "chee"). Traditional Chinese medicine states that the meridians work to flush out and nourish different tissues. Blood and nerve impulses also follow meridians throughout the body on their way to various organs.

If there is a block in any of the meridians, the energy, blood, and nerve impulses would not be able to travel their courses. The energy, blood, or impulse would begin to back up, sort of like cars in a traffic jam. This jam would also affect other meridians and throw the Yin and Yang out of balance. The blocked meridians can eventually lead to disease.

Acupuncture works by altering the body's energy, or Qi. By altering the Qi, the blocks and jams can be loosened and once again there can be harmony within the body.

Sterilized acupuncture needles, which are much thinner than a standard hypodermic needle, are inserted at specific points along the meridians. Chinese medicine believes that the needles tap into the body's Qi and reestablish the routes along a meridian.Thus acupuncture stimulates the body to heal itself.

Modern science explains the effects of acupuncture in a different way. Doctors and researchers believe that acupuncture needles stimulate the nervous system to release certain chemicals into the brain, spinal cord, and muscles. These chemicals may raise the threshold of pain within the body, thus making you feel better. Another theory is that these chemicals may let out even more chemicals and hormones. These chemicals and hormones work to monitor the body and regulate disorders or disease that may be present.

Somebody using acupuncture to treat disease would be considered cured when all meridians are unblocked, Qi is moving freely, and the Yin and Yang are working in harmony.

Massage Therapy

A deep, therapeutic muscle massage can actually stop a migraine attack. Muscle massage is often advised for people with chronic tension headaches, in addition to people plagued with migraines. This type of massage is given by a licensed professional massage therapist. Your doctor should be able to provide you with a recommendation.

A massage given by a licensed professional may only be a head and shoulder massage or could be a complete body massage. The type of massage given is normally dictated by your needs. The goal of a therapeutic massage is to diminish muscle tightness and pain and provide a general feeling of relaxation.

At the first sign of an impending headache, you may be instantly stressed, causing your neck and shoulders to tighten and your back to cramp. A severe migraine or headache can make you drop everything you are doing, often forcing you to leave school or work to deal with the pain. You may also have a fear of how long it's going to last, and how many more activities you might miss. This anxiety triggers the release of even more chemicals in the body that are associated with stress. These chemicals build up in your body. This buildup can cause tight muscle contractions.

Usually the massage is given in a darkened, quiet room. Soft music may be playing. It should be a serene, relaxed setting. If you have chronic headache pain, sometimes taking yourself out of everyday environments and going to such a nonstressful place can help to ease head pain.

Sometimes it is difficult to contact a professional for a massage. In these situations you can massage your own neck and head muscles during a headache. Often, this self-massage can help to ease head pain. Stretching the neck muscles before a massage can enhance the relief. You can stretch your neck muscles by slowly tilting your head side to side.

A massage is relaxing and can help ease any anxieties about head pain. Lessened anxieties, in turn, will help to promote more relaxed muscles. And loosened muscles can ease head pain and actually prevent future headaches. A total body massage also helps to reduce swelling of muscles. The easing of muscle tension usually leads to greater flexibility.

Deep muscle massages are beneficial to your emotional state. They are also helpful in ridding the body of built-up toxins in addition to easing tight muscles. Massages can lead to a general feeling of health and well-being.

There are many different massage techniques. Work with your massage therapist to find the one that's best for you. Tell them what you like and don't like and what brings relief to your headaches. Explore different options. If you don't feel comfortable with one therapist, try another.

Chiropractic Treatment

There is a debate over whether chiropractic treatments are an alternative form of medicine. Many people consider a chiropractor to be a medical doctor. Chiropractors do not attend traditional medical schools, but they do attend special chiropractic schools. They do not have a medical degree but chiropractors must be licensed in order to practice. Many chiropractors are also highly educated on different aspects of health and physical and emotional well-being.

Headaches are one disorder that chiropractic medicine has been very successful in treating. Some chiropractors specialize in headache and migraine treatment. A competent chiropractor could bring you tremendous relief from your pain.

Many people have pain in their necks or a "stiff neck," where they often can't tilt their heads very far in any direction. Chiropractic medicine believes that this stiff

124

neck is actually a symptom of a much larger problem within the spinal column. A chiropractic treatment can often provide more freedom of movement in the neck.

Chiropractic treatment involves the manipulation and adjustment of the spinal column to its proper alignment and the treatment of various disorders throughout the body. A misaligned spinal column is thought by chiropractors to be the cause of many different problems within the body, including headaches. The misalignment can compress or irritate nerves in the lower neck, as well as cause muscle contractions in the neck. Most important, chiropractors believe that when the spinal column is not in alignment, the joints in the neck don't fit together properly. If the neck joints don't fit properly, a headache can result.

In addition to manipulation of the spinal column, chiropractors use other techniques to help alleviate headache pain. These techniques include stretching exercises for the muscles of the neck and special contour pillows to relieve the strain put on the neck while sleeping. Chiropractors also use cold and heat therapy to combat swelling and irritation of inflamed muscles and joints. Sometimes chiropractors ask that you keep your neck perfectly still, or in traction, for a time. Or they may suggest that you wear a soft collar which may help relieve any nerve irritation. All of these methods have been known to be effective for people battling head pain. Remember to consult your doctor before starting a new treatment for your head pain.

Self-Help Methods and Relaxation Techniques

Evidence exists that both the ancient Egyptians and Aztecs had their own ways of relieving the pain of their headaches. Trying to relieve the pressure and pounding felt within their heads, they drilled into the patient's skull and cut away pieces of the bone. Records show that some of these patients actually may have survived the procedure. Whether the drilling gave them any headache relief is doubtful. Thankfully, today's treatments are not as drastic.

The first step in trying to control your headache and migraines should be a visit to your doctor. Sometimes it isn't very easy to get in touch with your doctor, particularly in the middle of a migraine. But reaching for medication every time you have a headache isn't always the best approach. This is when treatments that *you* control may prove helpful. If you try any treatment and you think it makes your pain worse, stop it immediately.

Sleep

Your body needs plenty of rest. Many people are so busy that they often get less sleep than their bodies demand. Too little sleep can contribute to many different ailments, including migraines and headaches. Sleep is also very important in maintaining a balanced emotional state. Think back to a morning when you had to go to school or work after getting very little sleep. You may not have felt well that morning, or you may have felt "out of sorts."

The most common and most successful of all treatments for tension headaches and common and classic migraines is sleep. Some doctors think that falling asleep allows the body to "reset" itself. Or, sleep may take the body out of its "headache mode" and into a healthy state. As little as a few minutes of deep sleep can greatly alleviate a headache and even make it disappear.

Unfortunately, when you are in the throes of a violent headache, falling asleep can be difficult. And if you do fall asleep, you may be awakened very early because of depression and anxiety over your headaches. The pain escalates when your body doesn't receive the sleep that it needs.

Luckily, the cycle of sleepless nights can be broken. The first step is to set a regular routine. Go to bed at a certain time and get up at the same time every morning. Do not nap during the day, even if you slept little the night before (unless the nap is to rid yourself of a migraine). Napping during the day can throw off your body's natural sleep rhythms.

Try to avoid any caffeine or alcohol close to bedtime. Both of these substances can alter the sleep cycle and contribute to headaches. Going to bed stressed or angry can also upset your sleep cycle. Try to clear your head or resolve any immediate problems before climbing into bed.

When you go to bed at night, make sure the room is as quiet and as dark as possible. You may need to wear earplugs or a sleep mask if your room is too noisy or bright. Make sure you have supportive pillows so your head rests comfortably. A pillow that is too firm can put a strain on neck muscles. Don't watch television or read a book while lying in bed. Close your eyes and try to relax.

It is best to try to fall asleep naturally. If you lie awake for twenty minutes with no hope of falling asleep, get out of bed and do something else, like read. It does not help to lie in bed and grow frustrated over your lack of sleep. A glass of milk has certain properties in it that can help to make you drowsy. Or you can practice relaxation exercises to make yourself more relaxed.

If your trouble sleeping seems to stretch on for more than just a few days, talk to your doctor. He or she may have some suggestions for you. Getting yourself into a regular sleeping routine is one of the first steps toward gaining control over your head pain.

Exercise

Physical exercise can actually help to prevent future migraines and other headaches, and a lack of it can leave you vulnerable to headaches. You do not have to train as if you're trying out for the Olympics, but you should exercise on a regular basis if you want any benefit from it. If you have any pain from the exercise, or your headaches actually become worse, then it is time to stop. Overexercise is not healthy. It is also important that you stretch your muscles before and after beginning any physical activity.

Walking, jogging, biking, and hiking are all great aerobic exercises that can be done with friends. At the very beginning of a migraine or other headache, try taking a brisk walk or go for a bike ride. Do this before the pain becomes intense. Exercising helps to get your blood pumping, which may prevent a lack of blood in the brain.

Exercise also helps to almost reverse the migraine process. During physical exercise, blood is rerouted from the head and scalp to other parts of the body, such as the arms and legs. This can prevent the blood vessels in your head from continually dilating and constricting, which is thought to contribute to the pain in your head. Exercise also raises the level of endorphins in the body, which are your body's natural painkillers.

Regular exercise may help to reduce the frequency, length, and intensity of migraines and other headaches. Regular exercise is a great way to reduce stress and tension. Exercise can also leave you with an overall feeling of health and more self-confidence.

Home Remedies

Most headache sufferers receive plenty of advice from family and friends on how to treat the pain. Every headache varies from person to person, and effective treatments also vary. What works for twenty other people may do nothing for you.

There is nothing wrong with trying a number of ways to relieve your headache. Some home remedies may work for you. And home remedies can even be better than always reaching for medication at the first sign of trouble. Remember: Check with your doctor before beginning any new treatments.

Coffee or Tea?

Strong tea or coffee can sometimes work to relieve headache pain. This is because they both can contain caffeine. Caffeine acts on blood vessels, helping to constrict swollen vessels that may be causing pain. Too much caffeine, however, can be a powerful trigger of migraines and other headaches.

Herbal teas have also been used as headache remedies. Many kinds have been used and have been shown to provide relief. Some herbal teas contain caffeine and others do not. In addition, drinks made from Brazilian cocoa and kola nuts are thought to be another headache remedy.

Other people have found headache relief by drinking water, fruit juices, and soft drinks. You should avoid alcoholic drinks, as they can bring about migraines and other headaches very quickly.

Nausea/Food

Most people suffering from migraines or other severe headaches can't stomach even the thought of food. Their nausea is so great that anything they eat probably won't stay down. For some people, having food in their stomaches may induce vomiting and bring relief.

For people who can eat during their headache attacks, food may help them to feel better. It may even shorten the length of the headache. Some foods that can be tolerated include toast, crackers, pasta, rice, potatoes, bananas, and cake.

If you are extremely nauseous but don't vomit, you may want to consider an anti-nausea medication. Some over-the-counter medications, such as Bonine and Dramamine, can be very effective in reducing nausea. Talk to your doctor about these medications.

Pressure

Applying light pressure to your head may bring some temporary pain relief. There is an artery running in front of both of your ears and through the temple. It may help to press on this bulging artery on the painful side of the head. Light pressure applied to the big artery found on your neck may also help to relieve a headache.

Ice/Heat

Both cold and heat have different properties that can be beneficial to headache pain. A simple act such as breathing in cold air can bring some relief.

Ice held on the base of the skull seems to work very well for many people with migraines and other headaches. Arteries at the base of the skull may be swollen and painful during a headache, and the ice works to reduce the swelling and stop any muscle spasms in the area. Ice also works to numb the area from pain. The ice can either be wrapped in a towel or you can use a gel pack that is stored in the freezer.

Some doctors believe that ice may also stop the release of certain chemicals responsible for the headache into the bloodstream. For people with mild to severe migraines, the ice may actually stop an attack. At the very least, it usually lessens head pain for most people.

Other people find that holding ice over their sinuses helps their headaches. A cold bath or shower can relieve pain. Putting one's feet in a cold foot bath may also bring relief.

Instead of cold or ice, some headache sufferers find relief from warmth. People with chronic headaches often discover that heat eases their pain. The same is true for people whose migraines last for more than forty-eight hours.

Heat works the opposite way than ice does. Heat opens blood vessels, so oxygen and other nutrients are able to travel through these blood vessels more easily and reach muscles. These nutrients can then speed the healing process.

A warm bath, heating pad, or electric blanket may help to end a headache. Heat packs, such as a heating pad or a warm, moist cloth applied to the back of the neck, have been proven to work for many people. A hot foot bath may also help, or, at the very least, be very relaxing.

Other Tips

Menthol creams and balms can help to ease head pain. When applied to your skin, menthol provides a feeling of coolness to the skin. Certain nerve endings, in the presence of menthol, are stimulated and send messages of "I'm cold" to the brain. The cold then acts as a sort of local anesthetic. If you have a tension headache or migraine located near your forehead or face, rubbing menthol on these painful spots may help.

Some doctors advocate the use of honey as a headache remedy. Studies have found that one tablespoon of honey eaten at the beginning of a headache or migraine attack can bring relief for some people within a half-hour.

Feverfew is a type of herb that is said to relieve migraines. Some people also claim that feverfew can prevent future migraines if the leaves are eaten every day. Feverfew leaves can be brewed with hot water and made into a tea, or it can be purchased in capsule form at health food stores. Check with your doctor before beginning a regime of feverfew to see if it is safe for you.

Relaxation Techniques

Some people don't like the idea of taking medications for their head pain, or any other discomfort. Instead, they try other techniques that use the power of the mind to control pain.

Biofeedback

You are fully aware and capable of controlling the external functions of your body on an everyday basis. You can command your foot to kick a soccer ball, or your fingers to pick up a pencil. But most people have no control over involuntary functions such as body temperature. Biofeedback is a technique designed to gain control over your body and its reactions and processes. It can teach you to gain some control over internal body processes.

The premise of biofeedback is that when people are aware of a bodily process, they can exert more control over that process. Machines and computers, run by a trained therapist, are used to monitor internal body workings. The machines are meant to allow you to see what is going on inside your body. The machines act like windows to your insides. Once you can see what is going on, you may be able to change some of your body's reactions. Then you would be able to tell which relaxation exercises are really working for you.

During biofeedback training, a therapist or psychologist will connect you to painless monitoring devices. A computer will also give readings on your level of muscle tension and body temperature.

The therapist will then show you different exercises that can control your level of muscle tension, your circulation, and your blood vessels. As you learn to relax different muscles, decrease your blood pressure, and slow your pulse, the machines will show you the effects within your body. As soon as you have mastered the relaxation exercises, the machines will no longer be needed.

Using biofeedback has been proven to reduce the severity and frequency of many migraines and other headaches. Once you have learned how to control some of your internal body functions with relaxation exercises, you should be able to reduce stress and head pain on your own. When you feel a migraine or other headache starting, you can override some of the functions that are acting out and causing pain.

Biofeedback can take many months to learn. For this reason, your doctor will probably keep you on headache medication until you have mastered the technique. Biofeedback also helps to relieve general anxiety and stress. There are no side effects.

Relaxation Exercises

Stress, one of the most common triggers of migraines and other headaches, comes in many different forms. You may become stressed when asked to say a few words after accepting an award. You may feel stress when preparing for a date. You will probably also feel stress when taking an exam. The stress may result in sweaty palms or a red face. Your breathing may become quicker and shallower. Stress can also trigger a headache.

The red face, sweaty palms, and headache are all due to the "fight or flight" chemical, or adrenaline, being released within your body. Adrenaline allows the senses to become heightened and more aware. Adrenaline also allows you to feel excitement.

Prolonged or repeated adrenaline responses, however, can lead to physical symptoms. These symptoms can include an elevated heart rate or chronic headaches. The more upset you become, the more adrenaline is released. Soon everything may feel like stress to the body and more and more adrenaline may be released.

If somebody feels a migraine attack coming they often become upset. Adrenaline begins to surge through the body. The migraine that was already coming is now compounded and even more painful. It's a vicious cycle. Relaxation exercises can help to rid the body of that extra adrenaline and calm the body and mind.

When you begin relaxation exercises, they should be practiced together with medications prescribed by your doctor. Relaxation exercises will help any medications to work more efficiently. Conversely, relaxation exercises may work better if you are taking medication to control some of the pain. One of the goals of relaxation exercises is to reduce or even eliminate the medication needed to control head pain.

Some people have found that after practicing relaxation exercises, the number of headaches they experience decreases. Relaxation exercises have been known to stop a migraine or headache already in progress. Many people also use relaxation exercises to prevent future migraines from happening. Relaxation exercises may also help you get rid of general nervousness and anxiety.

Many of the relaxation exercises involve intense focusing and concentration. This may be hard to do when your head feels like it is being pounded with a jackhammer. For this reason, it is important to master the exercises when you are feeling well.

Simple relaxation training is easy and can be done at home. Success of the technique is linked to how motivated you are to learning and applying what you learn. There are many books and audio tapes available at bookstores and libraries that can be helpful in learning more about relaxation. Some migraine and other headache sufferers may benefit from a few formal sessions with a psychotherapist trained in relaxation therapy. Following are some examples of relaxation therapies.

Deep Breathing

Deep breathing, or controlled breathing exercises, is one form of relaxation therapy. When you are stressed or upset, your breathing is usually fast and shallow. Fast, shallow breathing uses more muscles than relaxed breathing. When more muscles are used to breathe, it can lead to tense and tightened neck and shoulder muscles. These contracted muscles can aggravate a headache.

When you are relaxed, you breathe using your diaphragm, which is a muscle located near your stomach. Deep breathing exercises can teach you to relax and breathe using the diaphragm.

Deep breathing exercises are easy. Often, deep breathing can take the place of medication when you feel a migraine or other headache coming. Some people find that repeating a soothing word, such as "relax," helps them to concentrate even more on their breathing. The deep breathing can be practiced as follows:

1. Lie on your back in a comfortable spot. Place one hand on your abdomen and the other on your chest.

2. Breathe slowly through your nose. Try to use your diaphragm. The hand on your stomach should rise while the hand on your chest remains still. Concentrate on breathing calmly and deeply.

3. Inhale slowly, hold that breath for a few seconds, then slowly exhale. Continue to do this. Try to concentrate on being relaxed and breathing rhythmically.

It is a good idea to practice deep breathing when you are not suffering from head pain. Then you will be knowledgeable in how to control your breathing and it will be much easier to control your breathing when you are in pain. The exercises can be used either on a daily basis, as a way to prevent headaches, or when a headache occurs. Twenty to thirty seconds of deep breathing can sometimes get rid of a mild headache. If you are using deep breathing to rid the pain, you should begin the exercises as soon as you feel a headache coming. In this way, you have combatted your pain without having to reach for medication.

Progressive Muscle Relaxation

Progressive muscle relaxation is a therapy that can be done with very little training. It is a very relaxing and soothing exercise, and it may be able to ease the pain of a headache. As you concentrate on your various muscles, the focus will be shifted away from your head pain because your nervous system is fooled into concentrating on these muscles instead.

To practice progressive muscle relaxation, wear comfortable clothes and sit or lie on a comfortable surface. You may want to darken the room or play soft music. Close your eyes. You are going to concentrate on individual muscles, one at a time.

Starting with your toes and feet, contract the muscles. Hold those muscles tight for ten to twenty seconds. Then relax those muscle for thirty seconds to a minute. Next, focus on your calves. Tighten your calf muscles, then let them relax. Continue tightening different muscle groups of your body. After your calves, work on your thighs, buttocks, stomach, and chest. Each time you contract a muscle, focus intently on that muscle group. Then let the area relax completely. Continue contracting muscles in your hands, arms, and shoulders. Finally, contract the muscles in your neck, face, and scalp and then let them relax.

Continue the muscle relaxation exercise until you begin to feel some relief from your head pain. Try to concentrate and focus as intently as you can on the muscles. You want your body to think of something else besides the pain. Progressive muscle relaxation can be very effective if it is done carefully and correctly.

Guided Imagery
The goal of guided imagery is to trigger a reaction from the

brain in response to visualizing positive images. You are trying to get your brain to shift its attention away from head pain to something more pleasant. In other words, you want your brain to focus on something that does not hurt.

When doing guided imagery, you need to make yourself as comfortable as possible. Wear loose clothing. Sit or lie on a comfortable couch, chair, or bed. Close your eyes and imagine a calm, quiet scene. Visualize a place that relaxes you. It can be anywhere. Perhaps you enjoy lying on a warm beach. Perhaps floating in the clouds sounds calming to you. Begin the deep breathing. Relax. Picture yourself in the scene. Concentrate on all the details of the scene. Continue the deep breathing as you picture the scene.

It helps to practice guided imagery when you are feeling good. In this way, the exercise will come more easily to you when you are suffering from a headache. The better you become at guided imagery, the more focused you will be during the exercise. The more detailed your focusing scene is, the better your results.

Hypnosis

Hypnosis, or hypnotherapy, is an exercise that has helped people to relieve pain. Hypnosis is a very focused state of mind. A person in a hypnotic state appears to be sleeping.

In hypnosis, the mind is so focused that, in some cases, it is able to shift all attention away from pain. For people who are trained to hypnotize themselves, they are often able to stop headaches that are about to strike. This shifting of attention often aborts the headache or migraine.

Some people are also able to lower their own body temperature during hypnosis. This works much the same as reducing head pain by placing an ice pack on your neck. Lowering your body temperature is sort of like cooling the brain from within.

Self-hypnosis is not an easy thing to learn and takes practice to be effective. It is also much more difficult to perform with a blinding headache. Ask your primary care physician for a reference for someone who may be able to teach you hypnotherapy.

Helping Others

Anne

Anne wiped away her tears as she rang the door-bell at her neighbor's house. She was so upset. She waited for somebody to answer the door and wondered why her mom had yelled at her and told her to go next door and "leave her in peace."

Anne knew something was wrong with her mother as soon as she woke up. Her mom was usually awake long before Anne got out of bed, because she liked to work in the garden before breakfast. But when Anne walked into the kitchen to have breakfast, she could see the patch of flowers outside that her mom had said she was going to work on. They were still thick with weeds.

Anne poured herself a bowl of cereal. She had almost finished eating when her mom walked into the kitchen. She was still in her pajamas. Her eyes looked bloodshot and her face was pale.

"Mom, are you okay?" Anne asked.

"I'm fine," her mom snapped. "Why haven't you brought in the paper yet? Do you have to be so lazy?"

Anne was shocked. She and her mom had a great relationship. They disagreed sometimes, but they

141

were never mean to each other. Anne just hadn't thought about the newspaper. Her mom usually brought it inside each morning before Anne was even out of bed.

Anne quickly retrieved the paper from outside. When she walked back into the kitchen, her mom didn't even glance at the paper. She just sat at the table, staring out the window.

"Mom, are you okay?" Anne asked again. "Did you and Dad have a fight or something?"

"Why are you so nosy? I'm fine. Just leave me alone!" her mom yelled as she stomped out of the room.

Blinking back tears, Anne turned and picked up her dishes. When she was done washing them, she thought she would give it one more try with her mother. She didn't understand why her mom was acting this way.

Anne found her mother in the living room. She had closed all the shades and now sat on the couch in the darkness. Anne accidentally knocked over a vase as she entered the room.

"Anne! Why do you insist on being so loud! I have a pounding headache and I want it quiet!"

Her mom lay back on the couch. Anne just stood there. She couldn't believe her mom was yelling at her like this. It was just a stupid vase and it hadn't even broken. What had she done wrong?

"Anne," her mom said in a strained voice, "go next door. I want to be alone. Just leave me in peace."

Anne ran out of the house and across the yard. A simple headache wouldn't make her mom act like

142

that. Anne had had headaches before and they weren't anything to get that upset about. She must have done something really bad to make her mom so angry.

A Little Understanding

Someone in the middle of a full-blown migraine needs understanding. People with migraines and other severe headaches sometimes seem to undergo personality changes when they are in the middle of an attack. A normally pleasant, happy person may snap at you for seemingly no reason at all. A person with any type of headache is bound to be irritable.

Anne did nothing wrong to upset her mother. Her mother wasn't in control of her feelings at the moment and will probably feel bad for being so harsh with her daughter. But she is going to need Anne's understanding.

The best thing you can do for somebody in the middle of such a headache is to give her some peace and quiet. If she wants help, she will ask for it. Feeling sick is not very fun, and often people want to be left alone.

If someone close to you is prone to migraines or other severe headaches, your understanding of what they are going through is necessary. A migraine brings very real pain. No one wants to cancel planned events with family and friends and stay home feeling miserable. Someone with a migraine also probably feels guilty that she was the one to delay or cancel any plans. You need to reassure her that you understand and that you are there to help.

You can also help someone who is close to you learn how to avoid the headaches. Educate yourself about what she is going through. Ask her what you can do to make her life easier and less stressful. Just knowing that you understand and want to help may ease a great deal of stress in a headache sufferer.

Taking Charge

When a family member is stricken with a migraine or other severe headache, it may be up to you to take charge for a little while. The headache doesn't just affect the person who is sick; the whole family may feel its consequences. Assuming responsibility may be especially important if it is a parent or other adult who has the headache. You should be prepared to help the sufferer in any way you can.

Devise a plan with your parents about what to do if you suddenly need to take care of yourself or others. If you can, take charge of meals and other small household responsibilities while your parent is ill. You could help out by looking after your brother or sister. Stress the importance of peace and quiet for the headache sufferer.

Keep a calendar with each family member's daily activities listed on it. With the calendar, you will know how to get in touch with other family members, if necessary. Your family should also be able to get in touch with you.

Keep a list of emergency telephone numbers handy. Make sure the headache sufferer's doctor is on that list. Write down the name of any medications that the family member is taking next to the doctor's phone number.

There are many things you can do to help a migraine sufferer whether you're a family member or a friend. You may want to accompany the person on visits to the doctor. Going to the doctor can be frightening or overwhelming, and it's easy to forget or overlook things the doctor may have told you. It can help to have a second person there who is able to listen clearly to everything the doctor has to say. You can be that person.

You can also help a headache sufferer avoid triggers. If you are with that person a great deal and you know his or her triggers, you can plan activities and events where a headache is less likely to strike. You can also make sure any needed medication is brought whenever there is a trip or outing.

Exercise is a great way to prevent future headaches, and it's more fun to exercise when you're with a friend. You can go for a bike ride or a hike, or play a game of golf. Challenge your friend in basketball. Any activity that gets your heart pumping and allows you to have fun is good.

It is very important to be understanding to someone who suffers from headaches or migraines. Your understanding of the situation may help him or her to be a good friend to you if you ever experience headaches of your own.

Mastering Your Migraines

Tanya

Tanya stared at the clock on the wall, wishing that the hands would leap forward. She clenched her jaw tighter as she felt the first waves of a headache hit. Tanya could tell by the slow pounding that was beginning on the right side of her head that she was in for a major migraine. She glanced at the clock again. Class would be over in five minutes, and Tanya needed to take her migraine pill.

As the bell rang, Tanya stuffed her books into her bag and headed for the bathroom. On the way, she bought a bottle of juice from the vending machine. She walked into the bathroom and slipped into one of the empty stalls. Rummaging through her backpack, she remembered her doctor telling her that the Midrin would work better if Tanya took it at the very beginning of a migraine. As she washed down the pill with some juice, Tanya prayed that she had taken the pill in time. She just didn't have time for a debilitating migraine today.

As she sat in the bathroom waiting for the pill to work, Tanya tried to work on the relaxation techniques that her doctor had taught her. Dr. Yanez had explained that getting anxious or upset over an approaching migraine might actually cause the headache to be much worse than it otherwise would . Tanya closed her eyes and took several slow, deep breaths. She tried to breathe deeply from her diaphragm, and concentrate on inhaling from her abdomen. She continued her deep, slow breaths and started to feel her body relax. Tanya also felt for the first time that she was getting a handle on her headache.

Not wanting to rush things, Tanya stayed in the stall for a few more minutes. She thought about what could have brought on this headache. She hadn't gotten much sleep the night before because she had to study for a quiz. She had overslept and didn't have time to eat breakfast either. Tanya vowed that she would go to the cafeteria as soon as she felt better, and would eat breakfast from now on.

Coming to the conclusion that she was a migraine sufferer had been hard. Tanya remembered the times she lay on her bed in the dark and cried while her head pounded. Tanya's mom scheduled an appointment with the doctor when Tanya was forced to cancel plans and even miss school because of the pain.

Dr. Yanez asked Tanya a lot of questions about all sorts of things. He asked her about her eating and sleeping habits, what sort of medications she used, what kinds of stress she felt in her life, and whether or not she played any sports. Dr. Yanez also asked Tanya to describe exactly what her headaches were like. Then the doctor performed a short physical exam on Tanya, and ordered a series of blood tests.

At the end of the visit, Dr. Yanez told Tanya and her mother that he suspected that Tanya was suffering *from common migraines. He also talked to Tanya about triggers. Dr. Yanez explained that finding her own triggers may take some time, but that she should be patient and he was there to help her.*

Feeling much better, Tanya came out of the bathroom stall. Glancing at her watch, she noticed that she had only been in the bathroom for about fifteen minutes. Tanya was relieved and proud that she had helped herself avoid a major migraine.

"Tanya!"

Tanya looked over at the doorway; her best friend, Sandra, was waiting for her.

"Are you okay?" Sandra asked. "I've been looking for you! Do you want to go to lunch?"

Tanya smiled. "I'm just fine. Let's go!"

You can take control of your own body. It is possible to reduce and even eliminate your headaches. One of the keys to this goal is knowledge. Educate yourself. Gather as much information as you can about the type of headache or migraine with which you have been diagnosed. This knowledge will help you to better communicate with your doctor. Better communication can lead to a more precise treatment plan for your pain.

There are many different types of medication now available to help migraines and other headaches. Most of the over-the-counter medications are abortive drugs that can stop a headache in progress. Tension headaches and mild migraines often disappear with these types of treatments.

Severe tension headaches and strong migraines often need a prescription strength medication to diminish the pain. Prescription medication is only available through a doctor. If your headaches are becoming debilitating or are happening more and more often, you may want to consider prophylactic medications. These preventative drugs can stop future headaches from occurring.

You can make changes in your lifestyle that will reduce the frequency and severity of your headaches. Your doctor is always the first person you should talk to about any changes in treatments that you would like to make.

Working with Your Doctor

It is disappointing and frustrating when your life is changed because of head pain. But head pain can be controlled. Your doctor can help put your life back together.

Make an appointment with your doctor to talk about your headaches. Present your headache diary. Your head pain is serious and should be treated seriously. Discuss your headaches at the beginning of your appointment. If you only mention your head pain at the end of an appointment that was devoted to another health problem, your doctor may not think that your headaches are a problem for you, and your doctor may not make them a priority either.

The best treatment for migraines and other headaches is the one that works for you. Your doctor is knowledgeable about many different medications and methods of identifying and controlling pain. He or she is always learning about the latest treatments or will be able to refer you to someone who knows about them.

Tell your doctor if you are scared of the side effects of a certain medication. If you don't like to take medications, your doctor should know that right away. Speak up if you think a treatment is going to be too expensive for you. Ask your doctor for references if you think acupuncture, biofeedback, or any of the alternative therapies might be something that could work for you.

If you and your doctor decide that medication is the best way to treat your headaches, try to follow these guidelines:

- It may take a while to find the medication that works best for you; try to be patient.

- Follow the instructions for your particular medication; this will make it more effective.

- Avoid rebound headaches by only taking the right dose of your medication.

- Give any medication a trial period of a few weeks before deciding if it's a success or failure.

- If you are taking abortive medicines, be sure to take the medication at the very beginning of your headache. Don't wait until the pain is excruciating.

- Always keep your medication handy.

Make an effort to work with your doctor. Listen to all that he or she has to say. But also remember that you don't have to try every suggested treatment. It is your body and your health. You are in charge of it.

Headaches can be very painful, but they are not dangerous. To determine if you are suffering from a migraine or other common headache and not a different disorder, contact your doctor. If you develop headaches that are much more painful than usual or occur more often, make an appointment right away. Only your doctor is able to make a proper diagnosis and prescribe treatment.

Developing a Healthy Lifestyle

There are a few steps you can take that will lead you away from a life of headaches and towards a life of healthy living. Set up your own daily routine, and stick to it. Tell your friends and family about your routine, and let them know.

- ⇝ Eat three regular or five smaller, well-balanced meals at about the same time each day. Five small meals can help to keep sugar and other body chemical levels stabilized.

- ⇝ Keep track of your headaches and the foods you eat in your headache diary. Your diary can be an important link between you and your doctor in understanding your headaches and to pinpoint the foods to which you are particularly sensitive. Feel free to ask waiters in restaurants exactly what ingredients are used in certain dishes to help you avoid your triggers. Once you know your food triggers, you can avoid them.

- ⇝ Is stress the cause of your headaches? Assess the things in your life that are stressful to you. Decide if there is anything you can do about this stress.

151

For example, perhaps exams always trigger a headache. Maybe you could study with a friend before the exam to feel more confident and assured.

↪ Consider trying some relaxation techniques as a way to reduce your head pain. They can be used alone or in conjunction with headache medication. Ask your doctor to help you begin a biofeedback program. Take an instructional yoga class at your local fitness center. Learn how to better manage your time.

↪ Exercise is not only good for you, but it can help to relieve headaches. A regular exercise schedule of thirty to forty minutes three to five times a week can greatly reduce the frequency and severity of your head pain.

↪ Use sleep to your benefit and establish a sleep pattern. Go to bed at about the same time each night and get up at the same time each morning. Getting enough sleep and not oversleeping can help to regulate your body clock and reduce the possibility of another headache.

↪ Educate yourself and your family and friends about your particular type of migraine or headache. The more knowledge you have, the better you will be able to teach those around you.

↪ You may feel angry or depressed about your headaches. It may seem at times that you are the only one having to cancel plans and miss out on all the fun just because you're feeling sick. It's important to remember that you're not alone. There are people such as your doctor, friends, and family, who are there to help you.

Taking Back Control

Almost all sufferers of migraines and other recurring headaches feel a sense of anxiety. How much anxiety you feel and how much control your headaches have over your life is linked to your pain. If the thought of enduring another headache starts your heart pumping and your adrenaline rushing, you may be setting yourself up for another mammoth headache or migraine. Your emotional well-being—and a reduction in headaches—may lay in finding a way to control your anxiety about those headaches. You can find ways to take control of your headaches, and not let them take control of you.

Your own attitude is very significant in your treatment plan. Try to keep a positive outlook about your situation. Incorporate any lifestyle changes that reduce your headaches, and give medications or special therapies time to work. But don't forget to have fun and relax too. It may take some time and patience, but the long-term rewards are worth it!

Glossary

abortive medication Prescription or over-the counter drug that can stop or greatly relieve a headache or migraine in progress.

acupuncture A form of traditional Chinese medicine that uses the placement of very thin needles along specific places on the body that have been shown to relieve pain or other discomfort.

acute sinusitis An infection of the respiratory system that has settled into a sinus cavity.

adrenaline A chemical naturally produced in the body that stimulates heartbeat, raises blood pressure, and narrows blood vessels. Also called the "fight or flight" chemical.

antidepressants A class of medications that is typically used to treat depression but has also proven useful in treating migraines and other headaches.

aura A visual warning that a migraine is about to strike. An aura can be in the form of flashing lights, zigzag lines, dancing or shimmering colors, or other visual disturbances.

beta blockers Headache medication that works to stabilize blood vessels and control the release of certain chemicals within the body that may contribute to migraines and other headaches.

biofeedback A form of alternative medicine and stress reduction technique that teaches control over the symptoms of stress within the body.

butalbital compounds Prescription headache medications that combine barbiturates with painkillers.

154

calcium channel blockers   Medication originally used to treat heart problems but has also been shown to prevent headaches and migraines.

dilate   To swell or widen.

endorphin   A naturally produced painkiller occuring within the body.

ergotamine   A common medicine made from a fungus that is used to stop common and classic migraines.

hypoglycemia   A condition in which there is a sharp decrease of sugar in the blood.

neurologist   Doctor who specializes in the treatment of the nervous system.

neurotransmitter   A naturally produced chemical found in the brain that helps to convey messages and bridge the gaps between nerves.

NSAID   Nonsteroidal anti-inflammatory drug that works to prevent swelling of blood vessels and tissues within the body.

prodrome   A signal that a migraine is about to occur; a prodrome can include mood changes, a ringing in the ears, food cravings, or a cold feeling.

prophylactic medication   Prescription or over-the-counter drugs that work to prevent pain from ever occurring.

rebound headaches   A headache that is a result of the overuse of certain medications.

serotonin   A naturally produced chemical found in the brain that acts as a messenger and may play a role in migraines and other headaches.

trigger   A stimulus that can provoke a migraine or headache.

vasoconstriction   The narrowing of blood vessels that reduces the amount of blood, oxygen, and other nutrients that can pass through the vessel.

Where to Go for Help

American Council for Headache Education (ACHE)
875 Kings Highway, Suite 200
Woodbury, NJ 08096
(800) 255-ACHE
Web site: http://www.achenet.org

American Yoga Association
513 South Orange Avenue
Sarasota, FL 34236
(941) 954-3411
e-mail: yogamerica@aol.com

National Brain Tumor Foundation
785 Market Street, #1600
San Francisco, CA 94103
(800) 934-2873

National Headache Foundation
428 West St. James Place, 2nd Floor
Chicago, IL 60614
(800) 843-2256
fax: (312) 525-7357
Web site: http://www.headaches.org

National Institute of Neurological and Communicative
    Disorders and Stroke

National Institutes of Health
Building 3, Room 8A-O6
Bethesda, MD 20205
(301) 496-5751
Web site: http://www.ninds.nih.gov

Web Sites:

http://alt.support.headaches.migraine
Migraine support newsgroup where you are able to ask questions, receive support, and discuss your experiences with other migraine sufferers.

http://www.migrainehelp.com
Web site maintained by GlaxoWellcome, a pharmaceutical company, that offers a great deal of information on triggers, treatment programs, and an informative newsletter.

http://www.mayo.ivi.com
Web site maintained by Mayo Health Clinic that contains up-to-date information on a variety of health topics including migraines and other headaches. This site offers a searchable index.

Ronda's Migraine Page
http://www.msn.fullfeed.com/~ronda/
Web site maintained by a migraine sufferer. This site offers a journal of other sufferers' experiences, tips and advice, and many links to other headache sources.

For Further Reading

Duckro, Paul N., Ph.D., Janet E. Marshall, R.N., and William D. Richardson, M.D. *Taking Control of Your Headaches: How to Get the Treatment You Need.* New York: The Guilford Press, 1995.

Kandel, Joseph, M.D., and David B. Sudderth, M.D. *Migraine: What Works!* Rocklin, CA: Prima Publishing, 1996.

Lang, Susan S., and Lawrence D. Robbins, M.D. *Headache Help.* Boston: Houghton Mifflin Co.

Margolis, Simeon, M.D., Ph.D., medical editor. *Johns Hopkins Symptoms and Remedies: The Complete Home Medical Reference.* New York: Rebus, Inc., 1995.

Robbins, Lawrence D., M.D. *Management of Headache and Headache Medications.* New York: Springer-Verlag, 1994.

Theisler, Charles. *Migraine: Winning the Fight of Your Life.* Lancaster, PA: Starburst, 1995.

Index